HPBooks

GRILLING & BARBECUING

Tex-Mex Mixed Grill, page 30; Marge Poore's Texas Mop Sauce, page 108; Choddie's Mustard, page 116; and Grill-Baked Cornbread, page 150.

John Phillip Carroll & Charlotte Walker

John Phillip Carroll loves to barbecue because it's fun and it tastes good, and it fits the style of eating he likes most: "Good personal home cooking."

A California native, John began his food career in 1979 in the resort town of Mendocino working for Margaret S. Fox, owner of Cafe Beaujolais. This led to a two-year stint assisting various three-star chefs at Robert Mondavi Winery's "Great Chefs of France" cooking classes, in California's Napa Valley.

Through his association with Cafe Beaujolais he met and formed a lasting friendship with Marion Cunningham. A long-time colleague of James Beard, it was Mrs. Cunningham who guided the course of John's career. For two years, John and Marion directed the James Beard Cooking Classes on the West Coast. The past two years, John assisted Mrs. Cunningham with the testing and developing of recipes and material for the *Fannie Farmer Baking Book*.

Currently, John works as a private cook for a San Francisco couple, edits the San Francisco Professional Food Society newsletter and is a freelance writer.

Charlotte Walker grew up in the Southwestern United States where her family grilled year-round. A renewed interest in the subject of grilling and barbecuing was sparked after Charlotte researched and wrote a magazine article on the art of Smoke-Cooking Foods.

Charlotte received a B.S. in food and nutrition from Arizona State University and today is an accomplished food author, lecturer and consultant. She is the author of three cookbooks, including HPBooks' *Fish & Shellfish,* has written numerous magazine articles and is a regular contributor to the San Francisco Chronicle's food section.

As a lecturer, she conducts courses at the California Culinary Academy and the University of California's Berkeley Extension Division. She owns her own business, Charlotte Walker & Associates, which is a network of specialists providing creative services in the food area.

Active in food-related organizations, Charlotte is on the board of the San Francisco Professional Food Society and a member of Home Economists in Business, the International Wine & Food Society and the American Institute of Wine & Food. She has traveled extensively in Mexico, Europe and the Orient, and has participated in culinary-study trips to Mexico, Italy and Hong Kong. Currently, Charlotte makes her home San Francisco.

Published by HPBooks
a division of Price Stern Sloan, Inc.
11150 Olympic Boulevard, Suite 650
Los Angeles, California 90064
ISBN 0-89586-373-1
Library of Congress Card Catalog Number 86-80599
© 1986 Price Stern Sloan, Inc.
Printed in the U.S.A.

13 12 11 10 9 8 7

CONTENTS

ANOTHER BEST-SELLING VOLUME FROM HPBooks

Food Stylist: Sandra Griswold; Assistant Food Stylist: Kathy Briggs; Photography: Allan Rosenberg; Assistant Photographer: Allen V. Lott.

Acknowledgments: Paul Lapping, President, United American Food Processors, Chicago, IL; Stanley Kooyumjian, American Lamb Council; Gigi Pravada; Gayle Henderson Wilson; Myer's Community Council: Mary Murphy, Francine Yuelys; UNR Home Products; Sunbeam; Weber; Coleman; Paramount Housewares; Christen, Inc.; Anderson-Burley Woodside, Inc.: Mark Grimstvedt; Barbeque Council of America.

Cover Photo: Roasted Game Hens with Garlic Butter, page 73; Vegetable Brochettes, page 134; shrimp sautéed in Lemon-Parsley Butter, page 106; and Grilled Corn-in-the-Husk, page 137.

THE BASICS

Charcoal and wood cookery are the oldest forms of cooking known. Even before man used cooking vessels, he cooked in pits over slow fires. Historians have traced charcoal to the Neanderthal man. It is assumed that a burning log was covered by dirt or debris and left to smolder and burn. It was then dug up, relit and discovered to burn hotter, longer and with less smoke than fresh-cut wood.

Caribbean Indians adapted long, slow barbecuing as a means of preserving meat and fish in a damp climate. Early Spanish explorers, observing Caribbean green-wood-frame grills, named them *barbacoa*. Changes in spelling and pronunciation altered the word to modern-day *barbecue*.

The biggest boon to outdoor cooking in America came in the 1920s. Henry Ford invented charcoal briquets, a by-product of his wood-sided model "T" car. With the help of Thomas Edison, he designed a plant that burned wood scrap into charcoal. The charcoal was then ground, mixed with starch and formed into tight little "pillows"—the modern charcoal briquet.

Today, we're experiencing the culinary renaissance of barbecuing and grilling. Inventive young chefs have brought charcoal grilling into the restaurant. At the same time, there is an awakening of interest in old-fashioned down-home barbecuing.

DEFINITIONS

Grilling and barbecuing are confusing and often controversial terms. Even the way "barbecue" is spelled elicits heated arguments—Bar-B-Q, barbeque or barbecue? For the purpose of this book, we define the following terms.

A grill is the equipment used for cooking. **To grill** is to cook meat and other foods directly over heat, either on a wire rack or spit, to develop a crisp exterior and a succulent, juicy interior. Just about any food can be grilled—meat, fish, poultry, fruits, vegetables and breads.

A barbecue is an outdoor feast. **To barbecue** is to cook food in a covered grill, on a spit or in a pit, using a combination of heat and smoke. We have no pit barbecuing in this book. The key to traditional authentic barbecuing is slow, covered cooking over charcoal or hardwood. Barbecuing has countless ethnic, American regional, Asian and European variations.

Smoking is another confusing term. There are actually three methods of smoking food: cold-smoking, hot-smoking and water-smoking. In this book, hot-smoking and water-smoking are called *smoke-cooking*.

Cold-smoking smokes food at a low temperature for an extended period of time, often days or weeks, but does not cook the food. Cold-smoking is not covered in this book.

Smoke-cooking cooks and smokes food. **Hot-smoking** is essentially the same as our definition for barbecuing when wood chips or chunks are added to the coals to make smoke. **Water-smoking** is generally done in a water smoker, one of the more popular pieces of barbecue equipment on the market. The food is cooked in a smoky fog. Water or other liquid, such as wine, is held in the smokers' water-pan and helps keep the food moist. For more information on smoke-cooking, see page 12.

Curing was done before the days of adequate refrigeration, when cold-smoking was a means of preserving meat. Meat was cured before smoking with either a dry cure or brine. Curing retards the formation of bacteria and adds flavor as the dry cure or brine is absorbed by the meat. Today, meat that is smoke-cooked is generally not cured. We feel that marinades, bastes and sauces enhance the flavor of smoke-cooked foods and the smoked recipes in this book reflect this. However, for those who want to experiment with old-fashioned dry cures and brines, some recipes are given in *Sauces, Marinades & Butters,* beginning on page 100.

EQUIPMENT

Grills come in a range of sizes, shapes and styles—so many that it's hard to choose which to purchase. Many barbecue enthusiasts own several grills—one that is small and portable, another for smoke-cooking, and one for weekend feasting. The following is a brief description of the most common grills.

Open Charcoal Grills—Open grills can be purchased in many sizes, from small portable models for picnics or the beach, to large units that cook food for a crowd.

A round, portable brazier is the simplest and least expensive uncovered grill on the market. It is nothing more than a shallow metal pan fitted with a wire cooking rack, sometimes adjustable, and a draft door. These braziers lend themselves to grilling hamburgers, steaks, chops, fish and chicken pieces. Open braziers are not the best choice for cooking roasts, whole birds and thick pieces of meat unless you attach spit-roasting equipment. If you have an open brazier, you can make a foil tent to serve as a cover.

Hibachis are small portable braziers with limited grilling area, but they are ideal for one or two people, or for grilling hors d'oeuvres for a party.

Long, rectangular braziers, with a large grilling surface that cooks up to 60 steaks, can be rented.

Built-in indoor grills, constructed much like a fireplace, are nice, but few people have them. Fireplace grilling has received attention recently, but we do not recommend it. Grease can stain masonry, and a buildup of grease can create a dangerous a fire.

Homemade charcoal grills can be improvised with a little imagination and whatever you have on hand. You can use an oven rack balanced on two stacks of bricks, or chicken wire set over an old wheelbarrow. The only critical dimension is the distance from the top of the charcoal to the cooking rack, which should be adjustable from 4 to 6 inches.

Covered Charcoal Grills—The addition of a cover changes outdoor cooking from grilling to barbecuing or smoking. With a cover, you can achieve the low temperatures and smoky environment that's essential to true barbecuing. You can make your own foil grill cover, page 66.

Covered kettles are the most popular covered grills sold today. The cover turns the grill into an oven with radiant heat generated from the coals as it reflects off the inside surface of the cover. Because circulating hot air cooks food, you don't need a rotisserie.

Some covered kettles don't have an adjustable rack or grate. Internal temperature is controlled by opening and closing vents on the top and bottom, page 10.

Covered grills have the advantage of requiring less turning and watching of foods—and they use less charcoal. You can also save on fuel because the unused coals can be snuffed out by closing the vents. By using the cover and regulating the vents, you can avoid most flare-ups caused by fat dripping onto hot coals.

Some manufacturers recommend that you do all your grilling—even hamburgers, steaks and fish fillets—with the cover on during part of the cooking time. The open-grill recipes in this book can be adapted to this method if you desire. Use your owner's manual as a guide. Keep in mind that covered grilling may take 1/4 to 1/3 less time than open grilling, depending on the thickness of the food.

Rectangular and square grills with hinged covers work the same as covered kettles. You can regulate the temperature by moving the vents and adjusting the distance between the food and coals by either raising or lowering the cooking rack or charcoal grate. Some models are portable. Others are mounted on patio carts or permanently installed pedestals.

Kamados, which originated in Japan, are oval-shaped, covered grills made of heavy clay. Because clay is porous and holds the heat, the kamado is ideal for long, slow barbecuing and smoking.

Charcoal-Water Smokers—See page 12.

Gas & Electric Grills—Gas and electric grills are an increasingly popular alternative to charcoal grills. Some charcoal-barbecue enthusiasts claim that food does not attain that unmistakable outdoor woodsy quality due to the lack of charcoal or hardwood-fire smoke. However, gas and electric grills are easy to start, ready in 10 minutes or less and leave your hands clean.

Essential Barbecue Tools & Accessories

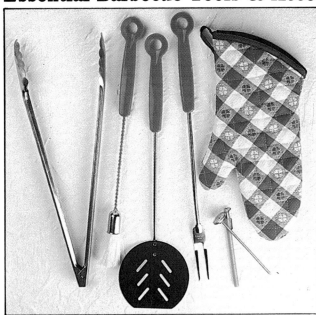

1/Long-handled tongs (to turn food), long-handled pastry brush, broad spatula, long-handled fork, heavy cooking mitt and rapid-response thermometer.

2/Stiff metal brush (for cleaning grill), long-handled tongs (to move coals), spritzer bottle (to spray down flare-ups) and charcoal chimney starter.

Recipes in this book can be cooked on any type of gas or electric grill. Allow the same amount of cooking time as on a charcoal grill. Use your owner's manual as a guide.

Most gas and electric grills are equipped with ceramic briquets, volcanic lava rocks or metal bars that deflect drips from falling on heating units. The barbecued taste comes from the flavor of the smoke produced by fat dripping and sizzling on the briquets, rocks or metal bars. To compensate for a lack of hardwood smoke, some manufacturers suggest placing soaked wood chips in a foil pan. Then place the pan directly over the heat. Consult your owner's manual for specific instructions.

Most gas and electric grills are lit by turning a dial or pushing a button, although some gas grills require using a match. Always open the cover when igniting the grill, then cover the grill to preheat it. Cook by the direct or indirect method, as you would in a charcoal grill, following instructions in your owner's manual.

Built-in countertop grills are produced by a number of kitchen range manufacturers. Food cooked on a countertop grill will have a wonderful flavor, but will not taste like it was cooked outdoors.

Portable electric or gas indoor-outdoor grills for the kitchen or patio offer year-round grilling.
Gas & Electric Smokers—See page 12.

GRILL CARE

After each use, scrape or scour the wire cooking rack with a wire grill brush, metal scouring pad, or crumpled foil. Grease and burned-on foods are easier to remove while the rack is warm. If you clean the rack immediately, it may never need to be cleaned with soap and water. Empty ashes from the fire-pan frequently.

Occasionally wash the inside and outside of the grill with soap and water. If the surface becomes heavily coated with soot and grease, give the grill a thorough cleaning with spray-on oven cleaner.

When not in use, store grill in a protected area, such as a garage. Or, cover the grill with an all-weather cover after it has cooled completely. Refer to your owner's manual for further instructions.

FUEL

There are several types of charcoal and aromatic wood to choose from. Experiment with different fuels that are available in your area to find the one, or combination, that best suits your taste and needs.

Store all charcoal and wood in a dry place. If you

Tools & Accessories

Essentials:

● Choose utensils with wooden or insulated handles. You may already have many of the necessary tools and accessories in your kitchen. We suggest you use what is on hand, but seriously consider buying long-handled tools when possible.

● You'll need two sets of **long-handled tongs,** one to move the coals and one to turn food. Spring-loaded tongs, rather than the scissor-type, are the easiest to handle.

● A **stiff metal brush** will make it easy to clean the cooking rack.

● Use a **long-handled fork** and **broad spatula** to assist in turning food.

● **Heavy cooking mitts** or **gloves** will protect your hands when you move the rack, turn a wire basket or open or close vents on a grill. Extra-long mitts give the greatest protection.

● Use a **long-handled basting brush** to apply sauces, butters and marinades. The mop-type used to wash dishes is also handy.

● For cooking meats, a **rapid-response thermometer** lets you read the internal temperature of food.

● You'll need a **drip-pan** to catch and hold juices and drippings that can be used for basting and sauces. A shallow, metal baking pan wrapped with heavy foil works well. Disposable foil pans or one you shape from foil, page 79, can also be used.

● Keep a **spritzer bottle** filled with water close to the grill to douse flare-ups.

● See **charcoal starters,** page 8.

● Use **heavy foil** to line the grill, wrap food, make drip-pans and covers.

Extras:

● There are times when a **hinged, rectangular grilling basket** is needed for foods that crumble and stick to the rack or require frequent turning. A hinged basket opens like a book and adjusts to the thickness of the food placed in it.

● If you grill much fish, you will want to own a **fish-shaped grilling basket** to grill whole fish.

● A **V-shaped rack** will hold roasts, ham, chicken and turkey on the cooking rack. The holder makes it easy to lift food.

● A **corn and potato holder** holds corn and potatoes around the edge of the cooking rack, leaving room to cook other food in the center.

● A **rib rack** doubles the rib-cooking capacity and allows even heat circulation.

● **Charcoal rails** keep charcoal away from the edge of the drip-pan.

● **Skewers** should be stainless-steel for meat kabobs or bamboo, if desired, for vegetables and hors d'oeuvres. Choose stainless-steel skewers with a flat blade so the food turns as the skewer is turned. Round skewers merely create a whole in the center of the food. Soak bamboo skewers 30 minutes before using to help prevent burning. For added support, and to help keep food stationary, thread food on two bamboo skewers spaced 1/4 to 1/2 inch apart.

● **Spit-roasting equipment** consists of a spit, a pair of tines that slide onto the spit at each end to hold food in place, and an electric motor. Spit-roasting baskets are also available.

● Charcoal must be kept dry. A **charcoal chest** has a spout for clean, convenient pouring and a removable top for filling.

● A **utensil rack** clips onto the edge of the grill to hold tools.

● If your grill is stored outdoors, use an **all-weather cover** to protect the grill.

● A **grill-surface thermometer** can be placed on the cooking rack above the coals to give an approximate temperature reading.

store it outdoors, keep it in a weatherproof container with a tight-fitting lid. Charcoal absorbs moisture easily and will not burn well if damp.

Charcoal briquets are the most commonly available and widely used fuel for grilling. Most are made from charred wood, coal, limestone and starch. However, briquets vary in quality. Some burn hotter than others, some burn longer and some start more easily. Good-quality briquets light easily and should be 80% covered with ash and ready to cook in about 30 minutes. They should burn at a moderate temperature about one hour. Poor-quality briquets are made from petroleum by-products. They feel greasy, smell strongly of motor oil and burn with a dirty smoke.

Instant-lighting briquets are impregnated with a chemical starter. Their advantage is that they light quickly and easily without the need for lighter fluid or other starters. If you use this product, be sure to let it burn at least 30 minutes before cooking.

Lump charcoal is produced by burning hardwood under special conditions to char it. It will then burn hotter, longer and with less smoke than dry raw wood. Many barbecue professionals prefer lump charcoal for these reasons and because it is available with no additives. However, lump charcoal is more expensive and harder to find than briquets. It also sparks and pops, so be careful when using it around buildings or shrubs. Lump charcoal has an irregular shape, which makes for an uneven, inconsistent fire. To compensate for this, break large chunks into smaller pieces.

Mesquite is the most popular and readily available lump charcoal, although oak, cherry, pecan, apple and hickory are found in many regions of the world. Mesquite and other hardwood charcoal are also available as briquets. The mystique of mesquite may be somewhat overblown. It's reputed to burn hotter and longer than most charcoal, hence its popularity for searing meats and cooking fish. It's aroma is light and pleasant.

Hardwood chunks, sticks and small logs can be used in your grill in place of charcoal. Hardwood burns very hot at first, then quickly dies down. The coals will not produce the same intense heat as charcoal, so the cooking time will be longer.

Aromatic hardwoods impart a distinct smoky, woodsy flavor to food. Avid barbecuers have strong regional preferences for the type of wood they use. Hickory is the most popular hardwood used. Its dense,

rich smoke imparts a rich, sweet flavor. But too much hickory is overwhelming and may make food bitter. Mesquite, favored in the American Southwest, has also gained international recognition. It has a milder, smokier flavor than hickory.

Aromatic woods can be purchased as chips, chunks or twigs. Wood pieces can be soaked in water before they are used, or can be used dry. Wet woods smolder and create maximum smoke. Dry woods burn rapidly and impart a milder flavor. Soak wood chips about 30 minutes, then squeeze out as much water as possible before adding them to the fire.

For an unusual and intriguing smoky flavor, toss bay leaves, garlic cloves, citrus peels or woody herbs, such as rosemary, sage or thyme, directly on the fire or place on the rack next to the food.

Do not use softwoods and evergreens, such as pine, cedar, spruce or fir. These resinous woods give off a bitter-tasting pitch that taints food and coats the inside of the grill with a sticky black film.

IGNITING CHARCOAL

To start a fire, use any of the approved methods below. Never use gasoline, alcohol or other highly volatile fluids because an explosion could result. If your grill doesn't have a charcoal grate, spread sand or gravel one inch deep over the bottom of the metal fire-pan. This permits a draft, letting the fire breathe.

To gauge the amount of charcoal needed, imagine the space the food will occupy on the grill. Use enough charcoal to cover this area plus one inch on all sides. An average fire will use 30 to 40 briquets.

The **charcoal chimney starter** is simple and easy to use to start a charcoal fire. All you'll need, in addition to the chimney, is a crumpled sheet of newspaper, a match and charcoal. To use the chimney, remove the rack from the grill. Place an 8-inch square of foil or a foil pie plate in the center of the charcoal grate or on sand or gravel. Do not set the chimney starter directly on the open grate or the draft will reduce the charcoal-starting effectiveness.

Crumple 1 to 1-1/2 sheets of newspaper and stuff into the bottom of the chimney starter. Fill the top with charcoal briquets. Set the chimney on the foil or pie plate and ignite the newspaper. Flames from the paper will ignite the charcoal. After 15 to 20 minutes or when the charcoal has begun to turn ash-gray, lift the chimney and remove the foil or pie plate. Then pour the hot charcoal onto the grate.

An **electric starter** is a simple metal loop that heats sufficiently to ignite charcoal briquets. It is a clean, easy way to start a fire; however, you must be near an electric outlet. Follow your owner's manual for using an electric starter.

Charcoal lighter fluid is the least-favored starter among experts and professional chefs. It is made from petroleum by-products and has a strong, objectionable odor. Many people feel that this odor permeates the food as well as the charcoal, and taints the flavor of the food. If you choose to use lighter fluid, pour the fluid generously over the charcoal. Let the starter soak into the coals before lighting it in several places with a match. Never add lighter fluid to a lighted fire or even to warm coals—it can cause flare-ups.

Wood-and-paraffin blocks are small solid blocks or sticks of compressed wood impregnated with a flammable paraffin. Place the blocks among pyramid-stacked charcoal; then ignite them with a match. As they burn, these odorless blocks light the charcoal around them.

You can use **kindling and newspaper** to start charcoal in a grill, just as you would start logs in a fireplace. The starters described above, however, are faster and easier to use.

In an open grill, food is grilled directly over a single layer of charcoal. If you're using lump charcoal, break it up into fairly uniform pieces. Ignite the charcoal as directed above, letting the charcoal burn 15 to 20 minutes or until the edges turn gray. With long-handled tongs, spread hot coals in a single layer. Arrange coals with hotter and cooler areas if space allows. See *Moving Coals,* page 10. Position the wire cooking rack in place to preheat. Wait another 10 to 15 minutes before cooking, until coals are ash-gray by day or glowing-red at night.

Manufacturers of covered grills describe two basic ways of cooking in a covered grill. The method you choose depends on the type of food you are cooking. **Direct Method**—This is the preferred method to use when cooking hamburgers, steaks, chops, sausage, chicken parts, fish and some vegetables. Open grill vents and remove the cover and cooking rack. Then follow the directions as outlined above for building a fire.

Indirect Method—With this method, food is cooked by reflected heat, not directly over coals. Food cooks slower than by the direct method. Use indirect heat for cooking large meats, such as roasts, turkeys, ham or whole chickens. Also use indirect heat for fatty meats, such as ribs and duck. Because there are no coals directly under the food, flare-ups and smoke are minimized.

There are two ways to prepare a grill for indirect cooking. For both, open grill vents and remove the cover and cooking rack.

Method 1: Position a drip-pan in the center of the charcoal grate. Place charcoal rails, if desired, on both sides of the drip-pan to hold coals away from the pan. If drippings will be used as a sauce or gravy, the rails will keep ash from falling into the drip-pan. Stack charcoal, pyramid-style, on each side of the pan, between the charcoal rails and fire-pan edge. Ignite the charcoal, page 8. In about 30 minutes, the coals will be ash-gray by day or glowing-red at night. Spread the hot coals around the drip-pan. Position the wire cooking rack in place to preheat. Then place the food on the rack over the drip-pan and cook according to the recipe.

Method 2: This is the method to use for the slowest cooking or when using a rotisserie. Position a drip-pan on one side of the charcoal grate. Place a charcoal rail on one side of the drip-pan to hold coals away from the pan, if desired. Stack charcoal, pyramid-style, beside the pan. Ignite the charcoal, page 8. In about 30 minutes, coals will be ash-gray by day or glowing-red at night. Spread hot coals on the grate beside the drip-pan. Position the wire cooking rack in place to preheat. Then place the food over the drip-pan and cook according to the recipe.

CONTROLLING TEMPERATURE

The most important rule in charcoal cookery is to allow enough time for the fire to get started properly before you begin cooking. It takes 30 to 40 minutes for the charcoal to reach the proper cooking temperature. In daylight, the coals will be covered with a layer of gray ash. At night, they'll have a red glow. This is when the coals are giving off the most even temperature.

Some covered grills are fitted with a temperature gauge. Grill-surface thermometers are also available. Or, use the unscientific hand-method temperature estimate described on page 10.

Adjust Rack Height—To quickly sear fish, hamburgers and steaks, lower the wire cooking rack for more intense heat. Raise the rack for longer, slower cooking without charring. In some charcoal kettle grills you cannot adjust the cooking-rack height. The only way to control temperature is by regulating air flow through vents.

Regulating Air Flow—Charcoal requires oxygen to burn. In a covered grill, vents located in the grill and cover control air flow. To raise the temperature or cook food faster, open the vents fully. If food is cooking too fast and you want to lower the temperature, close the vents halfway. To extinguish coals, close vents entirely. Use cooking mitts or hot pads to protect your hands when adjusting vents. Frequently remove ashes from the fire-box to keep vents from becoming clogged.

Moving Coals—How close the coals are to each other affects temperature. To lower temperature, spread coals apart so they don't quite touch. To raise temperature, bank coals together; with long-handled tongs, tap off the ash that doesn't flake off by itself.

You can create areas of "hot" and "hotter" in an open grill simply by clustering coals in one area and spreading them out in another area. This allows you flexibility to sear chops or steaks over the hottest coals, or cook them slower in a slightly cooler area.

Adding Charcoal—If you'll be cooking in a charcoal grill over one hour, replenish the charcoal after 45 minutes. **Do not use charcoal briquets that have been impregnated with starter fluid when adding more coals to an existing fire.** With long-handled tongs, add briquets to the edge of burning coals just before you start cooking. As long as the edges of the new briquets are touching burning coals, they will ignite. After 45 minutes, move these outer coals into the fire to maintain a constant temperature. Add more briquets to the edge of the burning coals; repeat this procedure up to the last 45 minutes of cooking.

Gas or Electric Grill—Temperature is easily controlled in gas or electric grills by adjusting the burner or heating element to a higher or lower setting.

Saving Coals—Because charcoal needs oxygen to burn, you can extinguish coals and reuse them by completely closing the vents in a covered grill. Or, lightly spritz the coals with water. Be careful with water because too much water on a hot grill can ruin the enamel finish. Partially burned coals don't burn quite as hot as unused briquets, so it's best to add new charcoal to the recycled ones each time you build a fire.

Whatever grill you use, cooking times in our recipes are approximate. A number of factors affect cooking time, including type of fuel used, distance of food from coals, size of the grill, outdoor temperature, size and temperature of foods being cooked, and whether you cook in an open or covered grill.

Take small pieces of meat from the refrigerator about 30 minutes before grilling. Large pieces should be removed up to an hour in advance. Keep meat covered or properly wrapped when not refrigerated. Meat cooks more quickly and evenly when it is not too cold.

Hand-Method Temperature Estimate

To get an unscientific temperature estimate, hold your hand, palm-side down, 2 to 3 inches above the cooking rack, until the heat becomes uncomfortable. The chart below shows how to judge fire temperature using your hand.

Heat Setting	Thermometer Reading	Time hand can be held over rack
High	375 and over	Hand over rack about 2 seconds
Medium	300 to 375	Hand over rack 3 to 4 seconds
Low	200 to 300	Hand over rack 5 to 6 seconds

Guidelines for Choosing a Grill

Ask yourself these questions before purchasing a grill:

- How many people will you serve?

  Grills come in all sizes, from hibachis for two to kettles and square covered cookers that can serve 12 to 20. For apartment balconies, boats, picnics and small families, the availability of small grills has never been better.

- What types of foods will you be cooking most?

  If grilling steaks is your style, look for a grill that needs a small fire. It will use less charcoal and be quicker to start than a large grill. If you savor the taste of smoked foods, consider a charcoal water-smoker—many can also be used as a regular charcoal grill.

- Do you want to slow cook in a gas grill?

  Then choose a covered gas grill that has low temperature settings necessary for slow cooking. Most grills do an adequate job on meats that cook fast at a fairly high heat, but not so well on foods that require long, slow cooking. These grills normally have low settings of 8,000 to 9,000 BTUs. A low setting of 6,000 BTUs is better for cooking chicken and pork without drying or burning the meat.

What features are worth considering?

- A heavy-duty porcelain finish is more durable and easier to clean than painted steel.
- A lid that tips back and stays in position while basting the food or adding coals is a handy feature on covered grills.
- An adjustable wire rack or charcoal grate helps control the temperature at which foods cook. A low position to sear meat and a higher position for longer cooking without burning is ideal. We have not suggested high, medium or low temperature in our recipes. If food is cooking too fast or becoming charred before it is time for it to do so, raise the rack or close the vents slightly, as explained on page 10.
- Look for a sturdy base to make the grill tip-proof, and wheels for easy portability.
- The cooking rack should have handles for picking it up and a space to add charcoal without moving the rack.
- An attached side table for setting mitts and tools is handy. Some removable metal or wooden racks are available. You can also use a separate worktable or cart.

Safety Precautions

- Never use a charcoal grill indoors. Be sure to locate the grill away from dry grass, bushes or other combustible materials.
- Never add starter fluid to hot or even warm coals. Flare-ups can be dangerous.
- Do not use kerosene, gasoline, alcohol or other volatile fuels to light charcoal because an explosion could result.
- Don't wear loose-fitting aprons, flowing sleeves or any article of clothing that could brush across the grill and catch fire. To prevent burns when tending the grill, use heat-resistant cooking mitts and long-handled utensils.
- With an open grill, use a spray bottle filled with water to douse flare-ups. Be careful to spray the water gently so food won't be covered with loose ashes. When using a covered grill, place the lid back on the grill and flames should die down.
- Cook fatty foods by indirect heat, as explained on page 9.

The most dependable way to know when meat is done is to use a thermometer. Internal temperature of large pieces of meat cooked in a covered grill can raise 5 to 10 degrees after it is removed from the grill. This is not true of a water-smoker. For perfect results, remove meat from the grill when it reaches a few degrees below the desired doneness temperature. See chart opposite. Cover the meat with foil and let it stand about 10 minutes. This allows the heat to balance out in the meat and the overall internal temperature to raise 5 to 10 degrees. Meat is also easier to slice after a brief standing time.

Smoke-Cooking

Although smoking as a means of preserving foods is done mainly in commercial smokehouses, backyard chefs are discovering how to smoke-cook in specially designed smokers. Charcoal, gas or electricity provide heat to cook food, while aromatic hardwood imparts a tantalizing smoky aroma and flavor.

Gas & Electric Smokers—These are mini versions of the kind of smokers used in many restaurants. Gas and electric smokers are fitted with a heating element in the bottom, a pan that is placed over the heat to hold smoldering hardwood chips and a wire rack above these to hold food. Recipes for smoked food in this book have been tested on a charcoal water-smoker, but they could be adapted to a gas or electric unit. Follow instructions in your owner's manual.

Homemade Smokers—For years, enthusiastic sportsmen and avid barbecuers have fabricated do-it-yourself smokers from garbage cans, barrels and old refrigerators. They have a heating element at the bottom, such as a hot plate; a container to hold the wood chips, such as a cast-iron skillet, and a rack for food. Homemade smokers may not be handsome, but most are as effective as store-bought models.

Water-Smokers—Portable water-smokers are the most popular and widely available type on the market today. Most water-smokers use charcoal as a heat source, but electric and gas models are available. A charcoal water-smoker consists of a heavy, dome-covered grill, fitted with a wire rack to hold food, and two pans—a fire-pan for charcoal and aromatic wood chips and one for water or other liquid. Large smokers come with two wire racks that make it possible to smoke quantities of meat for a crowd, or to cook both meat and vegetables at the same time. Most water-smokers are versatile enough to double as a covered barbecue grill, a steamer and an open brazier. Some water-smokers have a side door for replenishing charcoal and liquid with minimal loss of heat.

The use of water, wine, beer, fruit juice or any combination of liquids, makes smoke-cooking in a water-smoker different than other methods of smoking. Charcoal or a heating element heats the liquid, which creates steam that combines with wood smoke. This smoky fog cooks the meat, making it tender and juicy. This method results in slow, moist cooking without turning or basting. However, the food does not attain a crusty exterior.

Smokers vary from one brand to another. When you prepare these recipes, refer to your owner's manual for how much charcoal, liquid and aromatic wood to use.

See pages 6 and 8 for information on fuel and aromatic woods. Cut wood into 3-inch by 2-inch pieces, small twigs or chips, or purchase packaged wood chunks, sticks or chips where you find grilling equipment. Before adding packaged chips or small sticks to the smoker, soak them in water 30 minutes so they will burn slower and will smoke and smolder. Soak large chunks several hours. Use 1/4 to 1/2 pound wood chips or chunks for a lightly smoked flavor and 3/4 to 1 pound chips for a smokier flavor. Squeeze out excess water before adding soaked wood to hot coals.

Because chunks burn slowly, add all of them when you start smoke-cooking. Small sticks and chips burn more quickly, so add them at intervals during cooking. Don't overdo with flavoring woods—too heavy a smoke flavor gives food a bitter taste. Delicately flavored foods should be smoked with mild woods, such as mesquite, fruitwoods or grapevines. Hickory has a particularly assertive flavor. As you experiment with smoke-cooking, you will learn which woods you prefer with different foods, and you can use more or less wood to suit your taste.

For an interesting flavor, add four or five garlic cloves or four or five strips of lemon or orange peel to the charcoal. Or, add three or four large sprigs of a woody herb, such as rosemary, tarragon, sage or thyme.

Temperatures & Times for Grilling Meat

	Cut of Meat	When to Remove from Grill*	Temperature After Standing 10 Minutes†
Beef	Roasts		
	rare	130F to 135F (55C)	140F (60C)
	medium	150F to 155F (65C to 70C)	160F (70C)
	well-done	160F to 165F (70C to 75C)	170F (75C)
	Flank Steaks	10 to 16 minutes	
	Steaks (1 inch)	6 to 16 minutes	
	Burgers	8 to 15 minutes	
	Ribs	1 to 1-1/2 hours	
Pork, Fresh	Roasts	160F to 165F (70C to 75C)	170F (77C)
	Chops	12 to 15 minutes	
	Spareribs	70 minutes	
Pork, Smoked	Uncooked Ham	160F to 165F (70C to 75C)	170F (77C)
	Cooked Ham	130F to 135F (55C)	140F (60C)

*Cook all pork until well-done.

	Cut of Meat	When to Remove from Grill*	Temperature After Standing 10 Minutes†
Lamb	Roasts		
	rare	130F to 135F (55C)	140F (60C)
	medium	150F to 155F (65C to 70C)	160F (70C)
	well-done	160F to 165F (70C to 75C)	170F (77C)
	Chops (1 inch)	10 to 12 minutes	
	Ribs	30 to 60 minutes	

*Lamb is best when cooked rare or medium, but may be cooked well-done.

	Cut of Meat	When to Remove from Grill*	Temperature After Standing 10 Minutes†
Poultry	Turkey	10 to 15 minutes per lb.	180F to 185F (80C to 85C)
	Roasters	20 to 30 minutes per lb.	180F to 185F (80C to 85C)
	Broiler-Fryers		
	Whole	15 to 20 minutes per lb.	
	Cut-Up	15 to 20 minutes per lb.	

*For game, see specific recipes. Cook all poultry until opaque throughout.

	Cut of Meat	When to Remove from Grill*	
Fish	Fillets	7 to 10 minutes	
	Steaks (1 inch)	7 to 10 minutes	
	Large Whole Fish	20 to 60 minutes	
	Small Whole Fish	10 to 15 minutes	

*Cook all fish until opaque throughout.

†Large cuts of meat and poultry should stand 10 minutes before carving.

BEEF

Beef has been the favorite barbecue meat for as long as backyard grilling has been popular. Thick, tender Porterhouse steaks and sizzling, juicy hamburgers topped with a myriad of condiments remain the favorite barbecue fare.

Now is the time to venture beyond tender steaks and hamburgers and try your hand at tasty flank and skirt steaks. And don't stop there. Impress your friends and family with Texas-Style Beef Ribs; slow-cooked, marinated Grilled Tenderloin of Beef; and Hickory Smoked Brisket. Flank and rib steaks, though less tender than loin and sirloin, are as flavorful as other steaks.

Due to consumer demand, today's beef is leaner than ever before. However, lean beef tends to dry out more quickly on the grill. Marinating the meat will compensate for this. Many of the following recipes have suggested marinades. Use your imagination and experiment with other marinades.

For best results, disregard the time-honored prohibition against turning steaks more than once on the grill. Steaks turned only once tend to dry out quickly because much of the juice ends up either in the drip pan or on the coals. A steak will retain its juices better if you turn it occasionally as it cooks. Use tongs or a spatula to turn meat; forks puncture, allowing juices to escape.

If time permits, bring steaks to room temperature before grilling them to ensure even cooking. Trim off most of the fat; less fat means fewer flare-ups. Slash the remaining fat at 1-inch intervals and steaks won't curl as they cook. To determine if a steak is done, make a small slit in center of the meat.

Check doneness of larger cuts by using a meat thermometer. Remove large pieces of beef from the grill before they are completely cooked. Cover with foil and let stand about 10 minutes. Temperature will rise 5 to 10 degrees. For "before standing" and "after standing" temperatures, see page 13. After standing, meat will have maximum flavor and juiciness, and will be easier to cut.

Hamburger deserves the same care and consideration as the more expensive cuts of beef. By following a few simple guidelines, you can make perfect hamburgers on every occasion. First, purchase coarsely ground chuck. We feel that chuck has the best proportion of fat to lean beef. Then, be sure to handle the ground meat lightly because the less you handle it the more tender the burgers will be. You'll enjoy simple Basic All-American Burgers, page 26, served with condiments, or Roquefort Burgers, page 27, stuffed with an assertive cheese mixture.

Grilled Sirloin Steak

This is a fast, simple recipe using a tender cut of beef.

1 (2-lb.) beef sirloin steak,
  about 1-1/4 inches thick
Salt
Freshly ground black pepper
1 large garlic clove, minced

3 tablespoons fresh lemon juice
2 teaspoons finely chopped fresh
  oregano or 1 tablespoon finely
  chopped fresh parsley
1 or 2 lemons, cut in wedges

Preheat grill; position a wire rack 4 to 6 inches from heat. Sprinkle salt and pepper over both sides of steak; rub both sides with minced garlic. Place seasoned steak on rack. Grill 12 to 14 minutes for rare, 14 to 16 minutes for medium and 16 to 18 minutes for well-done, turning several times. Remove cooked steak to a carving board; sprinkle with lemon juice and oregano or parsley. To carve, cut steak in thin diagonal slices; arrange sliced beef on a warm platter. Serve with lemon wedges. Makes 4 to 6 servings.

Barbecued Chili Colorado

Barbecue the chuck roast first for added smoky flavor. Serve in bowls or over cooked long-grained white rice, or serve with warm tortillas and Mantequilla de Pobre, page 126.

1 (3-lb.) boneless beef chuck roast
Salt
Freshly ground black pepper
Red Sauce, see below
4 medium zucchini, cut in 1-inch slices
Water

1 (4-oz.) can ripe olives, drained,
  cut in wedges
1 (16-oz.) can golden hominy, drained
2 tablespoons chopped fresh oregano,
  if desired

Red Sauce:
2 tablespoons vegetable oil or bacon fat
1 medium onion, coarsely chopped
2 garlic cloves, crushed
2 (8-oz.) cans red chili sauce
3/4 cup tomato puree
1 (4-oz.) can diced green chilies

2 teaspoons ground cumin
1-1/2 teaspoons dried leaf oregano,
  crushed
1/2 teaspoon red (cayenne) pepper,
  if desired

Preheat grill; position a wire rack 4 to 6 inches from heat. Rub meat with salt and pepper; place on rack. Cover grill; open vents. Cook about 1-1/2 hours or until a meat thermometer inserted in meat registers 130F to 135F (55C) for rare, 150F to 155F (65C to 70C) for medium; turn every 15 to 20 minutes. Prepare Red Sauce, set aside. Cut zucchini into 1-inch slices; quarter each slice. In a medium saucepan, cook zucchini pieces in lightly salted boiling water 1 to 2 minutes or until crisp-tender. Drain; set aside. Remove cooked meat to a carving board. Cover with foil; let stand about 10 minutes. After standing, internal temperature of beef should register 140F (60C) for rare, 160F (70C) for medium. Cut cooked roast into 1-inch cubes; place in a 4-quart Dutch oven or deep pot. Add 1/2 cup water; bring to a boil, stirring occasionally. Add Red Sauce, cooked zucchini, olives and hominy. Cook 5 to 10 minutes or until heated through, stirring occasionally. Taste and adjust seasonings. Garnish with oregano, if desired. Makes 6 to 8 servings.

Red Sauce:
In a 2-quart saucepan, heat oil or bacon fat. Add onion; sauté 5 to 10 minutes or until soft. Stir in garlic; sauté 1 minute longer. Stir in chili sauce, tomato puree, green chilies, cumin and oregano. Bring to a simmer; simmer 10 to 15 minutes. Taste and adjust seasonings. Makes about 4 cups.

Marion Cunningham's Theatre Steaks

Once the preliminaries are taken care of, the grilling is done in a flash.

2 (8-oz.) beef loin tenderloin steaks,
   1-1/4 inches thick
1/2 cup butter or margarine
2 large onions, cut in thin rings
1/2 lb. fresh mushrooms, thinly sliced
Salt

Freshly ground black pepper
4 thick white-bread slices,
   preferably homemade
2 bunches watercress, rinsed,
   blotted dry, large stems removed

Trim fat from steaks. Cut each steak in half horizontally, making 4 steaks. In a large skillet, melt butter or margarine over medium heat. Add onions and mushrooms; sauté 5 to 7 minutes or until soft. Season with salt and pepper; keep warm. Preheat grill; position a wire rack 4 to 6 inches from heat. Place steaks on rack; sprinkle lightly with salt and pepper. Grill 1-1/2 to 2 minutes on each side; steaks should be rare. Place bread slices on grill 1 to 2 minutes before serving, turning once, until lightly toasted on both sides. Place each toasted bread slice on a warm plate; top with 1/4 of watercress and 1/4 of onion-mushroom mixture. Top each with a cooked steak. Press gently on each steak with a spatula, so warm juices drip down and watercress wilts slightly. Serve immediately. Makes 4 servings.

Barbecued Brisket Roll

You can make this ahead and freeze it until ready to use. To make great barbecued-beef sandwiches, place hot meat slices on small French rolls or hamburger buns; top with more barbecue sauce.

1 (3-lb.) beef brisket, trimmed,
   rolled, tied
Salt
Freshly ground black pepper

1 medium onion, sliced,
   separated in rings
1-1/2 cups All-American Barbecue Sauce,
   page 101, or other tangy barbecue sauce

Preheat grill; position a wire rack 4 to 6 inches from heat. Generously rub salt and pepper over surface of roast. Place seasoned roast on rack. Cover grill; open vents. Cook about 2 hours or until a meat thermometer inserted in meat registers 130F to 135F (55C) for rare, 150F to 155F (65C to 70C) for medium and 160F to 165F (70C to 75C) for well-done, turning meat every 15 minutes. Add more briquets every 45 minutes to maintain a constant temperature. Remove cooked meat to a carving board. Cover with foil; let stand about 10 minutes. After standing, internal temperature of beef should register 140F (60C) for rare, 160F (70C) for medium and 170F (75C) for well-done. To carve, cut and remove string. Cut meat diagonally across grain into 1/8-inch-thick slices. Keeping slices together, reshape roast; place on a warm platter. Scatter onion rings over top; brush roast and onions with barbecue sauce. Serve immediately or cool to room temperature. If roast will be served later, wrap cooled roast in a large piece of heavy foil, making airtight. Refrigerate up to 3 days or freeze until ready to use, up to 3 months. Thaw frozen meat in refrigerator overnight. To reheat, place foil-wrapped meat on a baking sheet; heat in a preheated 350F (175C) oven 30 minutes or until heated through. Makes 8 to 10 servings.

Marion Cunningham's Theatre Steaks; Pesto Tomatoes, page 134; and Minted Fresh Fruit Salad for a Crowd, page 157.

Teriyaki Flank Steak

This marinated steak becomes deep brown when grilled and is full of juicy flavor.

6 tablespoons soy sauce
1/4 cup dry sherry
1/4 cup vegetable oil
2 tablespoons chopped green onion

1 teaspoon finely grated fresh gingerroot
  or 1/2 teaspoon ground ginger
1 (1-1/2-lb.) beef flank steak

In a small bowl, combine soy sauce, sherry, oil, green onion and ginger. Place flank steak in a shallow baking dish large enough for it to lie flat. Pour soy mixture over steak; turn steak to coat both sides. Cover with plastic wrap or foil; refrigerate overnight or up to 2 days, turning meat occasionally. Remove meat from refrigerator 30 minutes before barbecuing. Preheat grill; position a wire rack 4 to 6 inches from heat. Remove meat from marinade, reserving marinade; pat off excess marinade with paper towels. Place marinated meat on rack. Grill 10 to 12 minutes for rare, 12 to 14 minutes for medium and 14 to 16 minutes for well-done, turning several times and brushing with reserved marinade. Remove cooked steak to a carving board. To carve, cut steak in thin diagonal slices; arrange sliced beef on a warm platter. Makes 4 to 6 servings.

Beef Pepper Steaks

These very tender steaks are coated with spicy black pepper, then quickly grilled.

4 (8-oz.) beef loin tenderloin steaks,
  1 inch thick
2 tablespoons vegetable oil
1 teaspoon salt

3 to 4 tablespoons black peppercorns,
  coarsely crushed
1 cup ketchup, if desired

Rub both sides of steaks with oil; sprinkle both sides with salt. Sprinkle pepper on both sides of each steak; lightly press into surface of steak. Let steaks stand 30 minutes at room temperature. Preheat grill; position a wire rack 4 to 6 inches from heat. Place steaks on rack. Grill 6 to 8 minutes for rare, 8 to 12 minutes for medium and 12 to 16 minutes for well-done, turning several times. Remove cooked steaks to a warm platter or individual plates. Serve with ketchup, if desired. Makes 4 servings.

Tuscan-Style Grilled Steaks

The seasonings provide a mild, tangy accent for a tender, flavorful cut of beef.

2 teaspoons freshly ground black pepper
1/2 teaspoon freshly grated nutmeg
1/4 cup olive oil
4 beef loin Porterhouse steaks,
  1 inch thick

2 tablespoons fresh lemon juice
1 lemon, cut in 4 wedges

In a small bowl, combine pepper and nutmeg; set aside. Using 1 tablespoon olive oil for each steak, rub oil onto both sides of steaks. Lightly rub pepper mixture over both sides oiled steaks. Sprinkle each steak with 1-1/2 teaspoons lemon juice; let stand 30 to 60 minutes at room temperature, turning once. Preheat grill; position a wire rack 4 to 6 inches from heat. Place seasoned steaks on rack. Grill 6 to 8 minutes for rare, 8 to 12 minutes for medium and 12 to 16 minutes for well-done, turning several times. Remove cooked steak to a warm platter; serve with lemon wedges. Makes 4 servings.

How to Make Stir-Fried Vegetables & Beef

1/When coals are hot use long-handled tongs to spread coals in a circle, leaving a small open space in center for wok. Using mitts, carefully set wok in open space in hot coals.

2/Quickly stir-fry meat; add fibrous vegetables first, like fennel and broccoli, which take longer to cook. Stir-fry remaining ingredients. After stir-frying, meat should be fork-tender and vegetables crisp-tender.

Stir-Fried Vegetables & Beef

Combinations of meat and vegetables are flexible, so use what you have on hand. Do not use a wood-handled wok.

2 tablespoons cornstarch
2 tablespoons soy sauce
1/4 cup water
1/4 cup vegetable oil or peanut oil
1 lb. beef sirloin, cut in 1-1/2-inch-wide, 1/4-inch-thick strips
3 fennel stalks, celery stalks or combination, sliced 1/4 inch thick
1-1/2 cups broccoli flowerets

1 green bell pepper, cut in thin strips
1 red bell pepper, cut in thin strips
2 zucchini or yellow crookneck squash or combination, halved lengthwise, sliced 1/4 inch thick
1 cup bean sprouts
2 or 3 leafy bok choy stalks, if desired, sliced 1/4 inch thick

Prepare all ingredients and have close to grill when you begin cooking. Stir-frying is a fast way to cook; actual cooking time is only 4 to 5 minutes. In a small bowl, combine cornstarch, soy sauce and water; set aside. Preheat grill; when coals are very hot, use long-handled tongs to spread coals in a circle, leaving a small open space in center large enough to hold wok firmly. Protecting your hands with cooking mitts, carefully set wok in open space in hot coals. Pour oil into wok; let stand 1 to 2 minutes until smoking hot. For well-done beef strips, add to hot oil and stir-fry 1 minute; for medium-rare strips, add as directed below. Immediately add fennel or celery to hot oil; toss constantly in hot oil 1 minute. Add broccoli; continue tossing 1 minute longer. For medium-rare beef, add beef strips at this time; toss in hot oil 1 minute. Add peppers and squash; toss 30 seconds or until crisp-tender. Stir in bean sprouts and bok choy, if desired. Stir cornstarch mixture; pour into beef mixture. Toss and stir 1 minute or until liquid thickens and forms a translucent glaze. Turn out onto a warm platter; serve immediately. Makes 4 servings.

Marinated Skirt Steak

A slightly peppery flavor permeates these quick-cooking skirt steaks. The slightly sweet marinade helps the meat brown nicely.

1 lime
1/3 cup dry red wine
1/3 cup soy sauce
2 garlic cloves, minced
2 tablespoons finely chopped onion

2 tablespoons molasses
1 tablespoon brown sugar
1/4 teaspoon hot-pepper sauce
1 (3-lb.) beef plate skirt steak

Grate peel from lime; juice lime. In a small bowl, combine lime peel, lime juice, wine, soy sauce, garlic, onion, molasses, brown sugar and hot-pepper sauce. Place steak in a shallow baking dish large enough for it to lie flat. Pour on marinade; turn to coat both sides. Cover with plastic wrap or foil; refrigerate 24 to 48 hours, turning occasionally. Remove meat from refrigerator 30 minutes before barbecuing. Preheat grill; position a wire rack 4 to 6 inches from heat. Remove steak from marinade, reserving marinade; pat off excess marinade with paper towels. Place marinated steak on rack. Grill about 6 minutes, turning once and basting frequently with reserved marinade. Steak should be served rare. Longer cooking will toughen steak. However, steak may be cooked 10 minutes for medium and 12 minutes for well-done. Remove cooked steak to a carving board. To carve, cut across grain in thin diagonal slices; arrange sliced beef on a warm platter. Makes 6 servings.

Orange-Glazed London Broil   Photo on page 103.

Cook flank steak just until medium. If overcooked it will toughen.

1 recipe Teriyaki Marinade, page 102
1 (1-1/2- to 2-lb.) beef flank steak
1/4 cup orange marmalade
Finely grated peel of 1 orange
    (about 1 tablespoon)

3 tablespoons fresh orange juice or
    lemon juice
2 tablespoons sugar

Prepare Teriyaki Marinade. Place flank steak in a shallow baking dish large enough for it to lie flat. Pour on Teriyaki Marinade; turn to coat both sides. Cover with plastic wrap or foil; refrigerate overnight or up to 2 days, turning meat occasionally. Remove meat from refrigerator 30 minutes before barbecuing. Preheat grill; position a wire rack 4 to 6 inches from heat. In a small saucepan, combine marmalade, orange peel, orange juice or lemon juice and sugar. Bring mixture to a simmer; simmer 5 minutes, stirring frequently. Remove beef from marinade; pat off excess marinade with paper towels. Place marinated meat on rack. Grill 10 to 12 minutes for rare, turning frequently and brushing with marmalade mixture during final 5 minutes of cooking. Steak should be served rare. Longer cooking will toughen steak. However, steak may be cooked 14 to 16 minutes for medium and 16 to 18 minutes for well-done. Remove cooked steak to a carving board. To carve, cut across grain into thin diagonal slices; arrange sliced beef on a warm platter. Makes 4 to 6 servings.

How to Make Grilled Tenderloin of Beef

1/Place meat in a dish so it lays flat. Sprinkle with onions and herbs. Pour on wine and oil; marinate tenderloin overnight for flavor to penetrate meat.

2/Pat off excess marinade with paper towel before barbecuing. Dust meat lightly with pepper and rub surfaces with oil.

Grilled Tenderloin of Beef

This is a luxurious treatment for an expensive cut of beef.

1 (3- to 4-lb.) fully trimmed
  center-cut beef loin tenderloin
2 onions, thinly sliced
2 bay leaves
4 whole allspice, coarsely crushed
2 teaspoons black peppercorns,
  coarsely crushed

2 tablespoon chopped fresh parsley
1/2 teaspoon salt
3-1/2 cups dry red wine
1/3 cup olive oil
1 tablespoon olive oil
Freshly ground black pepper

Place meat in a deep glass or ceramic dish. Sprinkle onions, bay leaves, allspice, crushed peppercorns and parsley over beef. Sprinkle with salt. Pour on wine and 1/3 cup olive oil; turn to coat evenly. Cover with plastic wrap; refrigerate overnight, turning meat and basting with marinade 3 or 4 times. Remove meat from refrigerator 30 minutes before barbecuing. Preheat grill; position a wire rack 4 to 6 inches from heat. Remove meat from marinade; pat off excess marinade with paper towels. Using 1 tablespoon olive oil, rub over all sides of meat; dust lightly with ground pepper. Place seasoned meat on rack. Grill 25 to 30 minutes or until a thermometer inserted in center registers 130F to 135F (55C), turning frequently to brown evenly on all sides. This cut should be served rare. Longer cooking will toughen meat; however, meat may be grilled until internal temperature registers 150F (65C) for medium and 160F (70C) for well-done. Remove cooked beef to a carving board. Cover with foil; let stand about 10 minutes. After standing, internal temperature of beef should register 140F (60C) for rare, 160F (70C) for medium and 170F (75C) for well-done. To carve, cut diagonally across grain into 3/4- to 1-inch-thick slices; place beef slices on a warm platter. Makes 6 to 8 servings.

T-Bone Steaks & Grilled Onions

A soft, melting mound of zippy blue cheese is a nice complement to a tender, well-flavored steak.

Blue-Cheese Butter, see below
2 large red onions, sliced 1/2 inch thick
1/4 cup olive oil
Salt

Freshly ground black pepper
4 (8- to 12-oz.) beef loin T-bone
** steaks, 1 to 1-1/2 inches thick**
4 large watercress sprigs

Blue-Cheese Butter:
1/4 cup crumbled blue cheese (1 oz.)
1/4 cup butter, room temperature

1 large garlic clove, minced
Several drops hot-pepper sauce

Prepare Blue-Cheese Butter; refrigerate until served. Brush onion slices with olive oil; sprinkle lightly with salt and pepper. Preheat grill; position a wire rack 4 to 6 inches from heat. Skewer onion slices on long wooden skewers; place on rack. Grill 3 to 5 minutes on each side until delicately browned but firm enough to hold their shape. Carefully move grilled onions to edge of rack to keep warm. Grill steaks 10 to 12 minutes for rare, 12 to 14 minutes for medium and 14 to 16 minutes for well-done, turning occasionally. Season lightly with salt and pepper after turning the first time. Remove cooked steaks and onions to individual plates; top each with 2 slices of Blue-Cheese Butter. Garnish each serving with a watercress sprig; serve immediately. Makes 4 servings.

Blue-Cheese Butter:

In a small bowl, combine all ingredients; shape into a 4-inch-long log. Wrap wax paper around log; refrigerate until firm. To serve, cut into 8 (1/2-inch) slices. Makes about 1/2 cup.

Variation

Substitute 4 boneless beef loin sirloin steaks, 1 to 1-1/2 inches thick, for T-bone steaks.

Barbecued Veal Chops

Be sure to buy veal loin chops because veal rib chops tend to fall apart on the grill.

4 veal loin chops, about 1/2 inch thick
Salt

Freshly ground black pepper
6 to 8 fresh oregano sprigs

Preheat grill; position a wire rack 4 to 6 inches from heat. Sprinkle veal chops with salt and pepper. Push 2 or 3 oregano sprigs through rack onto hot coals. Place seasoned chops on rack, cover grill. Cook 14 to 20 minutes to desired doneness, turning occasionally and dropping more oregano sprigs onto hot coals every few minutes. Remove cooked chops to a warm platter. Makes 4 servings.

T-Bone Steaks & Grilled Onions, and Grilled Tomatoes with Basil Vinaigrette, page 130.

Faujitas

This Mexican specialty cooks so fast it's good for a crowd, even if you have only one grill.

1 recipe Fresh Salsa from Fresh Salsa & Toasted Tortillas, page 123	**Salt**
2 lbs. beef plate skirt steak, flank steak or eye round roast or steak	**Freshly ground black pepper**
	2 or 3 limes, cut in wedges
1 recipe Mantequilla de Pobre, page 126	**12 or more (8- to 10-inch) flour tortillas, warmed**

Prepare Fresh Salsa. Place meat in freezer about 30 minutes until meat is partially frozen; partial freezing makes meat easier to slice thin. Meanwhile, prepare Mantequilla de Pobre; cover with plastic wrap, pressing wrap directly onto surface of Mantequilla de Pobre. Refrigerate until ready to serve. Preheat grill; position a wire rack 4 to 6 inches from heat. With a sharp knife, cut partially frozen steak in 1/4-inch-thick diagonal slices. Lay 2 or 3 slices in a single layer between pieces of plastic wrap. Using flat side of a meat mallet, pound until 1/8 inch thick. Be careful not to pound too thin or meat will shred. Repeat with remaining meat slices. Lightly season all pounded meat slices with salt and pepper. Place seasoned meat on rack. Grill 30 to 60 seconds on each side; these cook very quickly. Remove cooked meat to a warm platter. Let guests squeeze a few drops of lime juice over their grilled meat. Serve grilled meat with Fresh Salsa, Mantequilla de Pobre and tortillas. Makes 6 to 8 servings.

Texas-Style Beef Ribs

Soaked wood chips tossed on hot coals give these tangy beef ribs a mild smoky flavor.

2 (8-oz.) cans tomato sauce	**1 tablespoon Worcestershire sauce**
1/4 cup red-wine vinegar	**1/4 teaspoon red (cayenne) pepper**
2 tablespoons Dijon-style mustard	**4 to 6 lbs. beef chuck flanken-style**
1/4 cup lightly packed brown sugar	**ribs (back ribs), cut in slabs of**
2 garlic cloves, minced	**3 or 4 ribs each**

In a medium saucepan, combine tomato sauce, vinegar, mustard, brown sugar, garlic, Worcestershire sauce and red pepper. Bring sauce to a simmer; simmer 10 minutes. Generously brush ribs with sauce; reserve remaining sauce. Cover and let ribs stand 30 to 60 minutes at room temperature. Soak hickory chips or chunks in water to cover at least 30 minutes, using 1/4 to 1/2 pound chips for a lightly smoked flavor and 3/4 to 1 pound chips for a smokier flavor. Prepare and preheat grill for indirect cooking, page 6. Squeeze water from 1 or 2 handfuls of soaked wood chips; sprinkle on hot coals. Position a wire rack 4 to 6 inches from heat. Remove ribs from marinade; place on rack. Cover grill; open vents slightly. After 30 minutes, turn ribs; brush with reserved sauce. Cover and cook 30 minutes longer or until well browned, brushing once more with sauce. Remove cooked ribs to a warm platter. In saucepan, bring remaining sauce to a boil; pour into a serving dish. Serve separately. Makes 4 to 6 servings.

Beef Short Ribs, Oriental-Style

Meaty beef short ribs are brushed with an Oriental marinade.

2 tablespoons sesame seeds, lightly toasted
1 star anise
2 large garlic cloves, crushed
2 tablespoons grated fresh gingerroot
4 green onions with tops, finely chopped
1 teaspoon ground coriander
1 tablespoon sesame oil

1/4 cup sherry
1/4 cup soy sauce
1 teaspoon black peppercorns, coarsely crushed
4 to 6 lbs. meaty beef chuck short ribs (12 to 18)

In a small bowl, combine sesame seeds, anise, garlic, gingerroot, green onions, coriander, sesame oil, sherry, soy sauce and peppercorns. Place 1/2 of short ribs in each of 2 large heavy food-storage bags. Pour 1/2 of marinade into each bag. Press out air; seal bags. Squeeze gently, pressing marinade into meat. Set each bag in a large bowl; refrigerate 8 to 48 hours, pressing marinade into meat occasionally. Remove meat from refrigerator 30 minutes before barbecuing. Soak 2 or 3 handfuls of hickory chips or chunks in water to cover, at least 30 minutes. Prepare and preheat grill for indirect cooking, page 6. Squeeze water from soaked wood; sprinkle on hot coals. Position a wire rack 4 to 6 inches from heat. Remove ribs from marinade; place marinated ribs on rack. Cover grill; cook ribs 45 minutes, basting several times with reserved marinade. Add more briquets and soaked wood chips to maintain heat and smoke. Cover and cook 45 minutes longer, basting several times. Remove cooked meat to a warm platter; serve with parslied rice, fried rice or stir-fried vegetables. Makes 4 to 6 servings.

Veal Burgers

Lightly seasoned veal patties are low-calorie fare.

1-1/3 lbs. ground veal
Salt
Freshly ground black pepper

1 large garlic clove, crushed
Marge Poore's Barbecue Sauce, page 108

Preheat grill; position a wire rack 4 to 6 inches from heat. In a large bowl, combine all ingredients; do not handle meat too much or meat patties will be dense. Divide veal mixture into 4 equal portions; shape each portion into a thick patty. Place on rack; cook 5 to 7 minutes on each side or until slightly pink inside. Remove cooked patties to a warm platter. Serve immediately with Marge Poore's Barbecue Sauce. Makes 4 servings.

Basic All-American Burgers

Let guests assemble their own, adding condiments they desire.

2-1/2 lbs. lean ground beef
1 teaspoon salt
1/2 teaspoon freshly ground black pepper
2 large garlic cloves, minced
8 hamburger buns, cut in half horizontally
Ketchup

Mayonnaise
Dijon-style mustard or other mustard
2 large onions, sliced
2 large tomatoes, sliced
Iceberg lettuce leaves
Dill Pickles, page 118, sliced, or
    other sliced dill pickles

Preheat grill; position a wire rack 4 to 6 inches from heat. In a medium bowl, gently combine beef, salt, pepper and garlic. Do not handle meat too much or hamburgers will be dense. Shape seasoned meat into 8 round patties about 4 inches across and 3/4 inch thick. Place patties on wire rack. Grill about 8 minutes for rare, 12 minutes for medium and 16 minutes for well-done, turning once or twice. Move cooked hamburgers to edge of grill to keep warm. Place buns on rack, cut-side down, for 1 minute or until lightly toasted. Place warm hamburgers on toasted buns. Let each person use condiments they desire. Makes 8 servings.

Indonesian Ground-Beef Kabobs

A change of pace from plain hamburgers that will please kids as well as adults.

2 lbs. lean ground beef
2 eggs
1 teaspoon ground coriander
1 teaspoon ground cumin
1 teaspoon salt
1/2 teaspoon freshly ground black pepper
1/4 teaspoon red (cayenne) pepper

1/4 cup chopped fresh cilantro
2 garlic cloves, minced
2 tablespoons finely chopped green
    bell pepper
2 tablespoons finely chopped onion
16 oz. plain yogurt (2 cups)

Preheat grill; position a wire rack 4 to 6 inches from heat. In a large bowl, combine ground beef, eggs, coriander, cumin, salt, black pepper, red pepper, cilantro, garlic, bell pepper and onion. Shape mixture into small ovals about 1 inch in diameter. Thread ovals onto skewers or place in hinged wire grilling racks. Place skewers or hinged racks on rack. Grill 12 to 16 minutes, turning frequently to brown meat evenly on all sides. Remove cooked meat from skewers or hinged racks to a warm platter. Serve yogurt separately. Makes 6 to 8 servings.

How to Make Blue Cheese Burgers

1/Mash cheese and butter or margarine. Stir in walnuts, marjoram, and pepper; set aside. Prepare meat mixture and form it into patties.

2/Divide cheese mixture equally onto centers of 8 patties.

Blue Cheese Burgers

An unusual burger, filled with a rich, mellow mixture of blue cheese and walnuts.

1 cup crumbled blue cheese (4 oz.)
1 tablespoon butter or margarine,
  room temperature
1/3 cup chopped walnuts, lightly toasted
1 tablespoon chopped fresh marjoram or 1
  teaspoon dried leaf marjoram, crumbled

1/2 teaspoon freshly ground black pepper
2 lbs. lean ground beef
2 eggs
1/2 teaspoon salt

Preheat grill; position a wire rack 4 to 6 inches from heat. In a small bowl, mash cheese and butter or margarine together with a fork. Blend in walnuts, marjoram and pepper. In a medium bowl, gently combine beef, eggs and salt. Shape meat mixture into 16 round patties about 4 inches across and 1/4 inch thick. Do not handle meat too much or hamburgers will be dense. Divide cheese mixture equally onto centers of 8 patties. Top with remaining 8 patties; pinch edges together to seal in filling. Place filled patties on rack. Grill about 8 minutes for rare, 12 minutes for medium and 16 minutes for well-done, turning once or twice. Remove cooked patties to a warm platter. Makes 8 servings.

Border Burgers

Tangy open-faced burgers are topped with chili beans, chopped onion and grated cheese.

2 lbs. lean ground beef
1 (4-oz.) can diced green chilies
1-1/2 cups finely shredded Cheddar cheese
  (6 oz.)
1/2 teaspoon salt

1/2 teaspoon freshly ground black pepper
1/2 teaspoon ground cumin
4 hamburger buns, cut in half horizontally
2 (15-oz.) cans chili with beans, heated
2/3 cup chopped red onion

Preheat grill; position a wire rack 4 to 6 inches from heat. In a medium bowl, gently combine ground beef, chilies, 1/2 cup cheese, salt, pepper and cumin. Do not handle meat too much or hamburgers will be dense. Shape into 8 round patties about 4 inches across and 3/4 inch thick. Place patties on rack. Grill about 8 minutes for rare, 12 minutes for medium and 16 minutes for well-done, turning once or twice. Carefully move patties to edge of grill to keep warm. Place buns on rack, cut-side down, for 1 minute or until lightly toasted. Place a toasted bun half on each of 8 plates; top each with a cooked patty. Ladle about 1/2 cup warmed chili over top; sprinkle with a generous tablespoon each of cheese and onion. Makes 8 servings.

Barbecued Meat Loaf

Cook ahead as you barbecue other meat, then serve cold.

8 oz. ground lean beef
8 oz. ground lean veal
8 oz. ground lean pork
1 cup diced Swiss cheese (4 oz.)
1 medium onion, chopped
2 eggs, beaten

2 tablespoons chopped sun-dried tomatoes,
  packed in oil, drained, if desired
2/3 cup dry bread crumbs
1 cup milk
3/4 teaspoon salt
Freshly ground black pepper

Preheat grill; position a wire rack 4 to 6 inches from heat. In a large bowl, combine meats, cheese, onion, eggs and tomatoes, if desired. Stir in bread crumbs, milk, salt and pepper. Do not handle meat too much or meat loaf will be dense. Spoon meat mixture into a 9'' x 5'' loaf pan; place pan inside another loaf pan for insulation. Place pan on rack. Cover grill; open vents. Cook 1 hour and 30 minutes or until a meat thermometer inserted in center registers 160F (70C). Add more briquets after 45 minutes to maintain a constant temperature. Using heavy mitts or pot holders, carefully remove cooked meat loaf from grill to a carving board. Cover with foil; let stand about 10 minutes. After standing, temperature of meat loaf should register 170F (75C). Invert onto a warm platter, serve immediately or let cool completely. Wrap cooled meat loaf in foil; store in refrigerator until ready to serve. Serve chilled or at room temperature for wonderful sandwiches or picnic finger food. Makes 4 to 6 servings.

Border Burgers; Border Beans, page 131; and Macaroni Salad, page 140.

Tex-Mex Mixed Grill   Photo on page 1.

Here's a favorite dish from a fine California cooking teacher, Marge Poore.

1 recipe Marge Poore's Texas Mop Sauce,
    page 108
3 large garlic cloves, minced
3 tablespoons fresh lemon juice
1 (1-1/2-lb.) beef flank steak

4 large pork loin country-style ribs
    (1-1/2 to 2 lbs.)
4 to 6 German or Italian sausages
    (about 1-1/2 lbs.)

Prepare Marge Poore's Texas Mop Sauce; set aside. In a small bowl, combine garlic and lemon juice. Pierce surface of steak all over with a fork; rub lightly with about 1/2 of lemon mixture. Rub remaining lemon mixture onto ribs. Cut 3 (1/4-inch-deep) diagonal slashes in each sausage. Brush steak, ribs and sausages with a light coating of mop sauce. Place seasoned meats on a baking sheet; cover and let stand 30 to 60 minutes at room temperature. Meanwhile, preheat grill, building an especially large charcoal fire to accommodate this large amount of meat. Position a wire rack 4 to 6 inches from heat. Place seasoned ribs on rack; brush with mop sauce. Cover grill; cook 20 minutes. Turn ribs; place sausages on rack with ribs. Brush ribs and sausages with sauce. Cover and grill 20 minutes longer. Move ribs and sausages to outer edge of rack to keep warm. Place flank steak on center of rack; lightly brush steak, ribs and sausages with sauce. Turn steak after 5 minutes; brush with sauce. Cover and cook 5 to 7 minutes longer; steak should be pink in center. Longer cooking will toughen steak. However, steak may be cooked 2 minutes longer on each side for medium and 3 minutes longer on each side for well-done. Pork ribs should not be pink when cut in thickest portion not touching bone. Remove cooked meats to a carving board. To carve, cut steak across grain into thin diagonal slices. To serve, arrange ribs and sausages around outside of a warm platter. Arrange sliced beef in center of platter. In a small saucepan, bring remaining mop sauce to a boil. Pour into a serving dish; serve separately. Makes 6 to 8 servings.

Sweet & Sour Beef Saté

Well-seasoned but not too spicy, this skewered beef is delicious served over a mound of rice.

1 tablespoon plus 1-1/2 teaspoons
    tamarind paste
1 tablespoon plus 1-1/2 teaspoons water
2 teaspoons ground coriander
1 tablespoon chopped fresh parsley
3 garlic cloves, minced

1/2 teaspoon salt
2 tablespoons brown sugar
1-1/2 lbs. beef sirloin or loin,
    cut in 1-inch cubes
1 recipe Peanut Dipping Sauce, page 112

In a medium bowl, dissolve tamarind paste in water. Stir in coriander, parsley, garlic, salt and brown sugar; mixture will be thick. Add beef cubes; rub spice mixture into beef cubes. Cover with plastic wrap or foil; cover and let stand 30 to 60 minutes at room temperature or refrigerate 3 to 4 hours. If refrigerated, remove 30 minutes before barbecuing. Meanwhile, prepare Peanut Dipping Sauce; keep warm. Preheat grill; position a wire rack 4 to 6 inches from heat. Thread marinated beef cubes onto 6 metal skewers. Place skewers on rack. Grill 8 to 10 minutes or until meat is well-browned outside but still pink in center, turning frequently. Remove cooked beef from skewers; serve on a warm platter with Peanut Dipping Sauce. Makes 4 to 6 servings.

Smoked Hawaiian Short Ribs

Short ribs cooked for hours in a smoker result in tender meat which literally falls off the bones. Serve with ears of corn, Southwest Bean Salad, page 144, and pitchers of cold beer.

4 to 6 lbs. meaty beef chuck short ribs
  (12 to 18)
1 cup lightly packed brown sugar
1/2 cup cider vinegar
1 cup unsweetened pineapple juice

1/2 cup soy sauce
2 tablespoons dry mustard
1 to 1-1/2 cups All-American Barbecue
  Sauce, page 101

Place ribs, in a single layer, in a shallow baking pan. In a small saucepan, combine brown sugar, vinegar, pineapple juice, soy sauce and dry mustard. Stir over high heat only until sugar dissolves. Pour over ribs; turn to coat all sides. Cool, then cover and refrigerate 1 to 2 days. Soak oak or hickory chips or chunks in water to cover, at least 30 minutes, using 1/4 to 1/2 pound chips for a lightly smoked flavor and 3/4 to 1 pound chips for a smokier flavor. Build a charcoal fire in fire-pan of water-smoker or preheat as manufacturer directs. When coals are low-glowing and covered with a gray ash, spread out in fire-pan. Squeeze water from 1 or 2 handfuls of wood chips; sprinkle on hot coals. Place water-pan over coals; fill with water. Position a wire rack over water-pan. Remove ribs from marinade; set on rack above water-pan. Cover smoker; adjust vents as manufacturer directs. Smoke ribs 3 to 3-1/2 hours, brushing with All-American Barbecue Sauce 4 or 5 times. Add more briquets and soaked wood every 45 minutes to maintain heat and smoke; add more water to water-pan, if necessary, to keep it at least 1/2 full. Smoke until ribs are a deep, brownish red and meat pulls away from bones. Mound smoked ribs on a platter; keep warm. In a small saucepan, bring remaining All-American Barbecue Sauce to a boil; pour into a serving dish. Serve separately. Makes 4 to 6 servings.

Smoked Beef Ribs

These slow-cooked ribs served with a tangy barbecue sauce are finger-lickin' good. Serve with Old-Fashioned Coleslaw, page 144.

Double recipe All-American
  Barbecue Sauce, page 101
2 tablespoons Dijon-style mustard

2 teaspoon prepared horseradish
4 to 6 lbs. meaty beef chuck short
  ribs (12 to 18)

Prepare All-American Barbecue Sauce at least 1 hour before using. In a medium bowl, combine 2-1/4 cups barbecue sauce, mustard and horseradish. Cover and reserve remaining 2-1/4 cups barbecue sauce to serve with ribs. Place ribs in a single layer on a large baking sheet; spread mustard mixture over ribs, coating all sides. Cover and refrigerate 2 to 12 hours. Soak oak or hickory chips or chunks in water to cover, at least 30 minutes, using 1/4 to 1/2 pound chips for a lightly smoked flavor and 3/4 to 1 pound chips for a smokier flavor. Build a charcoal fire in fire-pan of water-smoker or preheat as manufacturer directs. When coals are low-glowing and covered with a gray ash, spread out in fire-pan. Squeeze water from 1 or 2 handfuls of wood chips; sprinkle on hot coals. Place water-pan over hot coals; fill with water. Position a wire rack over water-pan. Set ribs on rack above water-pan. Cover smoker; adjust vents as manufacturer directs. Smoke 3 to 3-1/2 hours. Add more briquets and soaked wood every 45 minutes to maintain heat and smoke; add more water to water-pan, if necessary, to keep it at least 1/2 full. Smoke ribs until meat pulls away from bones. Remove smoked ribs to a carving board; brush lightly with reserved barbecue sauce. Cut ribs into serving pieces; mound on a warm platter; keep warm. In a small saucepan, bring reserved barbecue sauce to a boil. Pour into a serving bowl; serve separately. Makes 4 to 6 servings.

Hickory-Smoked Brisket

Another less-expensive cut of beef, tenderized by long, slow cooking. We prefer to rinse off the salt cure before smoking. However if you prefer saltier meat with the flavor of corned beef, leave it on.

1 (5- to 6-lb.) beef brisket	**Double recipe All-American Barbecue**
1 cup Salt Cure for Meat, page 111,	**Sauce, page 101**
if desired	**Watercress sprigs or parsley sprigs**

Pat brisket dry with paper towels. If using salt cure, rub cure generously over surface of beef. Place salt-cure coated beef in a large heavy food-storage bag. Press out air; seal bag. Squeeze bag vigorously, pressing cure into meat. Set bag in a large bowl; refrigerate 2 to 3 hours, pressing cure into meat 2 or 3 times. If let sit overnight, beef will be very salty and will begin forming juices, making a brine. Meanwhile, prepare All-American Barbecue Sauce; set aside. Thoroughly rinse cured beef under warm running water; pat dry with paper towels. Set on a wire rack 30 to 60 minutes to dry. Soak hickory chips or chunks in water to cover, at least 30 minutes, using 1/4 to 1/2 pound chips for a lightly smoked flavor and 3/4 to 1 pound chips for a smokier flavor. Build a charcoal fire in fire-pan of water-smoker or preheat as manufacturer directs. When coals are low-glowing and covered with a gray ash, spread out in fire-pan. Squeeze water from 1 or 2 handfuls of wood chips; sprinkle on coals. Place water-pan over hot coals; fill with water. Position a wire rack over water pan. Place cured or uncured brisket on rack above water pan; brush lightly with barbecue sauce. Cover smoker; adjust vents as manufacturer directs. Smoke about 4 hours or until a meat thermometer inserted in meat, not touching bone, registers 130F to 135F (55C) for rare, 150F to 155F (65C to 70C) for medium and 160F to 165F (70C to 75C) for well-done. Add more briquets and soaked wood every 45 minutes to maintain heat and smoke; add more water to water-pan, if necessary to keep it at least 1/2 full. Baste 5 or 6 times with sauce during smoking. Remove cooked meat to a carving board. Cover with foil; let stand about 10 minutes. After standing, internal temperature of beef should register 140F (60C) for rare, 160F (70C) for medium and 170F (75C) for well-done. To carve, cut across grain into thin diagonal slices; arrange meat slices on a warm platter. Garnish with watercress or parsley. In a small saucepan, bring remaining barbecue sauce to a boil; pour into a serving dish. Serve separately. Makes 10 to 12 servings.

Barbecued Beef

Serving shredded beef in barbecue sauce is a great Southern tradition. Accompany with Charles Hall's Baked Beans, page 131, and Old-Fashioned Coleslaw, page 144, or on sandwich buns with mayonnaise and lettuce.

1 (3-1/2-lb.) beef rump roast	**Freshly ground black pepper**
1 garlic clove, cut in half	**2 cups spicy barbecue sauce**
Salt	

Preheat grill; position a wire rack 4 to 6 inches from heat. Rub roast on all sides with garlic; sprinkle with salt and pepper. Place seasoned roast on rack. Cover grill; cook 2 hours or until a meat thermometer inserted in meat, not touching bone, registers 165F to 170F (70C to 75C). Meat must be very well done to shred easily. Add more briquets every 45 minutes to maintain a constant temperature. Remove cooked meat to a carving board. Cover with foil; let stand about 10 minutes. After standing, internal temperature of beef to be shredded should register 175F to 180F (75C to 77C). Peel away any tough crusty exterior. With 2 forks, pull meat into shreds. Place meat shreds in a saucepan. Add barbecue sauce. Bring to a simmer; simmer 3 to 5 minutes or until bubbly and heated through. Makes 6 to 8 servings.

How to Make Prime Rib Roast Cooked in Coals

1/Brush outside of roast with mustard coating; place meat on a rack. Place rack over a baking sheet lined with foil. Pat salt into mustard; reuse all excess salt which falls onto foil.

2/Protect hands with mitts. Using 1 or 2 long-handled forks, lower meat into circle of coals. Using long-handled tongs, bank a row of hot coals around roast.

Prime Rib Roast Cooked in Coals

This results in an amazingly tender, flavorful roast.

1 (7- to 8-1/2-lb.) beef 3-rib roast, large end

1/2 cup Dijon-style mustard
About 2 cups coarse salt or kosher salt

About 4 hours before serving, trim fat from roast; pat roast dry with paper towels. Brush outside of roast with a generous coating of mustard. Pat as much salt as possible into mustard, turning roast to coat all sides. Set seasoned meat aside on a wire rack 30 to 60 minutes to dry; pat more salt on any moist or bare spots. Build a large charcoal fire in grill. After 30 to 40 minutes, when coals are very hot, spread out coals, clearing a space in center large enough to hold roast. Protecting your hands with oven mitts, carefully place seasoned roast, rib-side down, in open space among coals. With tongs, bank a row of coals around roast, with coals barely touching side of roast. Cover grill; cook about 2 hours or until a meat thermometer inserted in meat, not touching bone, registers 130F to 135F (55C) for rare, 150F to 155F (65C) for medium and 160F to 165F (70C to 75C) for well-done. Add more briquets every 45 minutes to maintain a constant temperature. Remove cooked meat to a carving board. Cover with foil; let stand about 10 minutes. After standing, internal temperature of beef should register 140F (60C) for rare, 160F (70C) for medium and 170F (75C) for well-done. Crack off salt coating, using paper towels to protect your hands; roast will be very hot. Rub outside of roast with a clean, stiff brush to remove as much salt and ash as possible from crevices. It is impossible to remove every trace of salt and ash; if desired, cut off outside layer from roast. To carve, cut across grain into thick slices; arrange sliced beef on a warm platter. Makes 6 servings.

Burgers au Poivre

This is less expensive than pepper steak to prepare, but we think just as good.

2 lbs. lean ground beef
2 tablespoons Dijon-style mustard
2 tablespoons Worcestershire Sauce

1 teaspoon salt
2 garlic cloves, minced
1/4 cup black peppercorns, coarsely cracked

In a medium bowl, gently combine ground beef, mustard, Worcestershire sauce, salt and garlic. Do not handle meat too much or hamburgers will be dense. Shape meat mixture into 4 to 6 large oval patties, 4 to 5 inches long, 3 inches across and 1/2 to 3/4 inch thick. Using 1 tablespoon crushed pepper for each patty, press pepper into both sides of each patty. Cover with plastic wrap; let stand 30 minutes at room temperature or refrigerate 3 to 4 hours. Remove meat from refrigerator 30 minutes before barbecuing. Preheat grill; position a wire rack 4 to 6 inches from heat. Place patties on rack. Grill about 8 minutes for rare, 12 minutes for medium and 16 minutes for well-done, turning once or twice. Remove cooked patties to a warm platter. Makes 4 to 6 servings.

Grilled Calves Liver

Cook liver over a hot fire so it's nicely browned outside and just pink on the inside.

4 (6-oz.) calves liver steaks,
    1/2 inch thick
1/4 cup olive oil
1/4 cup red wine
2 large garlic cloves, minced

1/2 teaspoon salt
1/2 teaspoon freshly ground black pepper
2 large red onions, sliced 3/8 inch thick
1 recipe Mustard-Herb Butter Sauce,
    page 109, if desired

Place liver steaks in a single layer in a shallow baking dish. In a small bowl, whisk together olive oil, wine, garlic, salt and pepper. Pour over liver; cover and let stand at room temperature 30 to 45 minutes. Preheat grill; position a wire rack 4 to 6 inches from heat. Place skewered onions on rack; grill 6 to 10 minutes or until delicately browned but still firm enough to hold their shape, turning occasionally. Carefully move grilled onions to edge of rack while grilling liver. Remove liver from marinade, reserving marinade; pat dry with paper towels. Place marinated liver on rack. Grill about 4 minutes, turning and basting with reserved marinade. Remove cooked liver to a warm platter; serve with grilled onions and Mustard-Herb Butter Sauce, if desired. Makes 4 servings.

PORK

From spicy ribs to succulent roasts, pork offers a variety of cuts that grill deliciously. Today, pork is younger, leaner and more tender than ever before. Select fresh pork with a fine firm texture and a moderate amount of marbling. The color may range from a grayish pink to a delicate rose.

Pork roasts, such as Honey-Mustard Glazed Pork Roast, Barbecued Pork with Green Peppercorns and Pork Tenderloins with Plum Sauce, will be juicier and more flavorful when cooked over medium heat. A meat thermometer is your most accurate guide to judging the doneness of a large pork cut. Let large pork roasts stand 5 to 15 minutes after grilling to allow juices to set and make carving easier.

Check doneness of larger cuts by using a meat thermometer. Remove roasts from the grill when they register 160F to 165F (70C to 75C). Cover with foil and let stand about 10 minutes. Temperature will rise 5 to 10 degrees. Pork must be cooked well-done to be safe, but don't cook it until it is dry.

Country-style ribs are the meatiest of all pork ribs. Spareribs have only a thin covering of meat, hence the name "spare." Plan on 3/4 to 1 pound ribs per person and about 1/4 cup barbecue sauce per pound of ribs.

Flare-ups are unnecessary and dangerous. To prevent flare-ups when cooking fatty cuts of meat, use a drip pan directly beneath the meat. The pan will catch the drips and keep them away from hot coals. If using a covered grill, cooking with the cover on will also keep flare-ups to a minimum.

Pork Hash

Pork gives a slightly smoky flavor to this old-fashioned favorite.

2 tablespoons butter or margarine
1 small onion, finely chopped
3 cups diced cooked pork
3 cups diced cooked potatoes
1/2 teaspoon salt

1/2 teaspoon freshly ground black pepper
1/4 cup bacon drippings or
   additional butter or margarine
1/3 cup whipping cream

Preheat grill. When coals are hot; position a wire rack 4 to 6 inches from heat. Place a medium cast-iron skillet on rack. Melt 2 tablespoons butter or margarine. Add onion; sauté 5 to 10 or minutes until onion is soft. Remove sautéed onion to a large bowl. Stir in pork, potatoes, salt and pepper. Heat bacon drippings or 1/4 cup butter or margarine in skillet. Spread meat mixture over bottom of skillet, pressing down firmly with back of a spatula. Fry mixture about 10 minutes, giving the pan a sharp jerk occasionally so hash doesn't stick. When hash has crusted slightly on bottom, scrape crust up and stir in. Press down again with a spatula; cook 10 minutes longer. Lift up an edge of hash; if bottom isn't forming a crust, place over hotter coals. Cook a few minutes longer; stir in crust again. Pour cream over top; press down firmly. Cook 15 minutes or until underside is well-browned. Carefully invert skillet over a large warm platter. If any hash sticks to pan, scrape out with a spatula and press into place on surface of hash. Makes 4 servings.

Variation
Substitute diced cooked chicken or lamb for pork.

Pork-Fried Rice

A hearty and flavorful dish with a Chinese influence, cooked in a wok over hot coals.

1/4 cup peanut oil or other vegetable oil
4 cups cold cooked long-grain white rice
8 to 10 mushroom caps, thinly sliced
1/2 to 1 cup chopped green onions
1 cup or more diced cooked pork

1/2 teaspoon freshly ground black pepper
2 eggs, slightly beaten
2 tablespoons soy sauce
2 tablespoons chopped fresh parsley

Prepare all ingredients and have close to grill when you begin cooking. Stir-frying is a fast way to cook; actual cooking time is only 4 to 5 minutes. Preheat grill; when coals are very hot, use long-handled tongs to spread coals in a circle, leaving a small open space in center large enough to hold wok firmly. Protecting your hands with cooking mitts, carefully set wok in open space in hot coals. Pour oil in wok; let stand 1 to 2 minutes until smoking hot. Add rice and mushrooms; stir and toss constantly in hot oil about 2 minutes. Add green onions, pork and pepper. Stir and toss about 1 minute. Move rice mixture to side of wok; pour eggs into cleared side of wok, stirring briskly about 1 minute until lightly scrambled; do not mix into rice mixture. Stir soy sauce into scrambled eggs; toss with rice mixture. Immediately turn out onto a warm platter. Garnish with chopped parsley. Makes 4 servings.

Variation
Substitute cooked tiny shrimp or diced cooked chicken or beef for pork. If desired, add 1/2 cup diced celery with green onions.

Glazed Baked Ham

A picnic ham is a cured, smoked and fully cooked pork shoulder. Its flavor is superb.

1/3 cup honey
2 tablespoons dry mustard
1 tablespoon Worcestershire sauce

1 tablespoon ground ginger
1 (5- to 8-lb.) fully cooked smoked
  pork shoulder picnic ham

In a small bowl, combine honey, dry mustard, Worcestershire sauce and ginger; set aside. Prepare and preheat grill for indirect cooking, page 9; position a wire rack 4 to 6 inches from heat. Remove any strings or cheesecloth covering ham. Use a sharp knife to cut 1/2-inch-deep crosshatch marks, about 1 inch apart, on fat-side of ham. Place ham on rack above drip pan. Cover grill; open vents fully. Cook 1 hour; brush surface of ham with honey mixture. Repeat brushing with honey mixture every 20 minutes for remaining cooking time. Cook 1 to 1-1/2 hours longer or until a meat thermometer inserted in center of ham, not touching bone, reaches 125F to 130F (50C to 55C). Add more briquets every 45 minutes to maintain a constant temperature. Remove cooked ham to a carving board. Cover with foil; let stand about 10 minutes. Cut into thin slices; arrange on a warm platter. Makes 6 to 10 servings.

Canadian Bacon in a Cheese Crust

Canadian bacon is made from boneless eye of pork loin and is much leaner than regular bacon. Like the picnic shoulder above, Canadian bacon has been fully cooked.

2 tablespoons prepared mustard
1 tablespoons water
1-1/2 cups all-purpose flour
1/2 teaspoon salt

2/3 cup vegetable shortening
1 cup finely shredded Cheddar cheese
  (4 oz.)
1 (2-lb.) piece unsliced Canadian bacon

Prepare and preheat grill for indirect heating, page 9; position a wire rack 4 to 6 inches from heat. In a small bowl, combine mustard and water; set aside. In a medium bowl, combine flour and salt; use a pastry blender or fork to cut in shortening until mixture is crumbly, light and dry. Stir in cheese; stir in mustard mixture. Stir briskly with a fork until dough makes a rough ball. Turn out dough onto a lightly floured surface; roll and pat out dough to a 13'' x 9'' rectangle. Place bacon in center of rolled-out dough. Fold up edges of dough, pressing firmly together and enclosing bacon completely. Place dough-wrapped bacon in a 9- or 10-inch cast-iron skillet. Place skillet inside another skillet for insulation. Place stacked skillets on rack. Cover grill; open vents fully. Cook 45 to 60 minutes or until crust is well-browned. Remove skillets to a heatproof surface. Using a spatula, lift baked bacon log to a rack; let stand about 10 minutes. Crust will crumble slightly when cut. To serve, carve into thin slices. Makes 6 to 8 servings.

Sage-Smoked Pork Chops & Applesauce

Cook the applesauce on the grill along with the chops.

Chunky Applesauce, see below
4 pork center-cut loin chops,
   about 1 inch thick

Salt
Freshly ground black pepper
Several fresh sage sprigs

Chunky Applesauce:
2 lbs. tart red cooking apples
1/2 cup water
1/4 cup sugar
2 tablespoons fresh lemon juice

2 tablespoons butter or margarine
1/4 teaspoon ground cloves
1/4 teaspoon ground cinnamon

Preheat grill; position a wire rack 4 to 6 inches from heat. Prepare Chunky Applesauce. Rub both sides of chops with salt and pepper; place seasoned chops on rack. Place sage sprigs on rack beside chops. Cover grill; cook pork chops 15 minutes or until no longer pink inside, turning occasionally. Cook slightly longer if you like pork well-done. Remove cooked meat to a warm platter. Garnish with fresh sage. Serve pork chops with Chunky Applesauce. Makes 4 servings.

Chunky Applesauce:
Cut apples into 1/2-inch chunks. Place in a heavy saucepan suitable for cooking on a grill. Add water, sugar, lemon juice, butter or margarine, cloves and cinnamon. Place on grill; cook 30 minutes or until apples are tender, stirring occasionally and adding more water only if there is no liquid in pan. Drain any excess liquid from cooked applesauce; stir with a fork to break up apples slightly. Sauce will be coarse. Taste and adjust seasonings. Spoon cooked applesauce into a serving dish. Makes 3 cups.

Lemon-Caraway Pork Chops

Caraway seeds give these chops a gamelike flavor. Serve with hot applesauce, horseradish & Old-Fashioned Coleslaw, page 144.

6 pork top loin chops, 1 inch thick
1/3 cup fresh lemon juice
1/3 cup olive oil
2 teaspoons dried leaf tarragon, crumbled

1 teaspoon caraway seeds
1 garlic clove, finely chopped
1/2 teaspoon salt
1/4 teaspoon freshly ground black pepper

Arrange chops in a single layer in a shallow baking pan. In a small bowl, combine remaining ingredients to make a marinade; pour over chops. Cover and refrigerate 8 hours or overnight. Remove meat from refrigerator 30 minutes before barbecuing. Preheat grill; position a wire rack 4 to 6 inches from heat. Remove chops from marinade; pat off excess marinade with paper towels. Place drained chops on rack. Grill 20 minutes or until outside is well-browned and center is still juicy, but no longer pink, turning once or twice. Cook slightly longer if you like pork very well done. Remove cooked chops to a warm platter or individual plates. Makes 6 servings.

How to Make Ginger-Plum Grilled Pork

1/If purchased from a butcher shop, boneless pork shoulder will be tied to hold pieces together. Remove string from rolled roast, if necessary.

2/On thick side of roast, make 2 deep, slanting cuts, starting from top and slicing to bottom, but not through bottom. You should end up with 2 flaps.

Ginger-Plum Grilled Pork

Long marinating is a good way to tenderize a less costly roast.

1 (3-1/2-lb.) boneless pork shoulder
  blade roast
1/2 cup plum jam
1/3 cup soy sauce

1/3 cup honey
1 teaspoon ground ginger
2 large garlic cloves, minced
1/4 teaspoon freshly ground black pepper

Remove strings from rolled roast, if necessary. Place roast on a flat surface. One side, or *lobe,* will be larger and more rounded than the other side. Make a deep, slanting slash through each side, cutting from top to bottom, but not all the way through, creating a flap. Fold flaps open; meat should measure 2 to 3 inches thick throughout. In a medium bowl, combine plum jam, soy sauce, honey, ginger, garlic and pepper. Place pork in a large heavy food-storage bag; add marinade. Press out air; seal bag. Squeeze gently, pressing marinade into meat. Set bag in a large bowl; refrigerate 2 to 3 days, pressing marinade into meat once or twice each day. Remove meat from refrigerator 30 minutes before barbecuing. Preheat grill; position a wire rack 4 to 6 inches from heat. Remove meat from marinade; pat off excess marinade with paper towels. Place marinated pork, with flap open, on rack. Grill about 1 hour or until a meat thermometer inserted in center of meaty portion reaches 160F to 165F (70C to 75C). Add more briquets after about 45 minutes to maintain a constant temperature. Remove cooked pork to a carving board. Cover with foil; let stand about 10 minutes. After standing, internal temperature of pork should register 170F (77C). To carve, cut across grain into thin diagonal slices; serve on a warm platter. Makes about 8 to 10 servings.

Honey-Mustard Glazed Pork Roast

Mustard, honey and ginger make a sweet yet spicy golden-brown glaze when grilled. Serve with Grilled Corn-in-the-Husk, page 137, or Corn Casserole, page 138.

1/3 cup honey
2 tablespoons finely grated orange peel
1/3 cup fresh orange juice
1/4 cup old-style prepared mustard
   with seeds or Coarse-Ground Mustard,
   page 114

1 teaspoon minced fresh gingerroot or
   1/2 teaspoon ground ginger
1/2 teaspoon salt
1/4 teaspoon red (cayenne) pepper
1 (3-1/2- to 4-lb.) boneless pork top
   loin roast, tied

In a small bowl, combine honey, orange peel, orange juice, mustard, ginger, salt and red pepper; set aside. Prepare and preheat grill for indirect cooking, page 9. Position a wire rack 4 to 6 inches over drip pan. Place roast on rack. Cover grill; open vents slightly. Cook roast 45 minutes; turn meat. Add more briquets to maintain a constant temperature. Brushing with honey mixture about every 10 minutes, cook 45 minutes longer or until pork has just a slight tinge of pink when cut into thickest part and registers 160F to 165F (70C to 75C) on a meat thermometer. Remove cooked pork to a carving board. Cover with foil; let stand about 10 minutes. After standing, internal temperature of pork should register 170F (77C). To carve, cut across grain into thin diagonal slices; serve on a warm platter. Makes 8 to 10 servings.

Grilled Pork, Mexican-Style

Cubes of tender barbecued pork and a spicy avocado dip are combined for a Mexican treat.

1 recipe Mantequilla de Pobre, page 126
1-1/2 to 1-3/4 lbs. pork loin tenderloin,
   cut in 1-inch cubes
Salt
Freshly ground black pepper

1 or 2 limes, halved
8 or more (8- or 10-inch) flour tortillas
   or 4 or more (7- or 8-inch) pita-bread
   rounds, halved, warmed
Dairy sour cream

Preheat grill; position a wire rack 4 to 6 inches from heat. Prepare Mantequilla de Pobre; refrigerate until served. Thread pork cubes on long metal skewers; sprinkle with salt and pepper. Place skewers on rack. Turning frequently, grill 20 minutes or until well-browned and meat is no longer pink in center. Remove grilled pork cubes from skewers; squeeze lime juice over top. Place about 5 cooked pork cubes on each tortilla or inside each pita half. Spoon on a few tablespoons of Mantequilla de Pobre. Roll tortillas around filling. Serve with sour cream. Makes 5 to 6 servings.

TIP *Cook most meats over medium coals or heat. A hot fire contributes to dryness and toughness of meat.*

Honey-Mustard Glazed Pork Roast; Skewered Potatoes, page 136; and Coarse-Ground Mustard, page 114.

Barbecued-Pork Sandwiches

An ideal recipe for group cook-outs or picnics as it can be multiplied easily.

1 (2- to 2-1/2-lb.) boneless pork
  top loin roast, tied
Salt

Freshly ground black pepper
Red-Wine Barbecue Sauce, see below
6 sourdough rolls or hamburger buns

Red-Wine Barbecue Sauce:
2 tablespoons vegetable oil
2 onions, finely chopped
1-1/2 cups ketchup
1 cup dry red wine
1/2 cup lightly packed brown sugar

1/3 cup red-wine vinegar
2 tablespoons Worcestershire sauce
2 tablespoons Dijon-style mustard
1 tablespoon chili powder
1/2 teaspoon salt

Preheat grill; position a wire rack 4 to 6 inches from heat. Season pork roast with salt and pepper. Place seasoned roast on rack. Cover grill; open vents slightly. Cook 45 minutes; turn meat. Add more briquets to maintain a constant temperature. Cook 45 minutes longer or until a meat thermometer inserted in center of roast reaches 160F to 165F (70C to 75C). Meanwhile, prepare Red-Wine Barbecue Sauce; keep hot. Remove cooked roast to a carving board. Cover with foil; let stand about 10 minutes. After standing, internal temperature of pork should register 170F (77C). Let stand covered 10 minutes longer for easier slicing. To carve, cut across grain into thin diagonal slices. Reposition rack about 4 inches from heat or preheat oven to 350F (175C). Lay a double thickness of heavy foil on barbecue rack or in a broiler pan. Place pork slices on foil, grouped in 5 or 6 overlapping slices; generously brush with sauce. Cook on grill or in preheated oven 15 minutes or until meat is nicely glazed, turning groups of sliced meat every 3 or 4 minutes and brushing with sauce. Move glazed meat to one side of foil; fold other side of foil over top to keep meat warm. Move foil-covered meat to side of grill or remove from oven; keep warm. Split buns or rolls; toast on rack, or toast in oven broiler until lightly browned. Make sandwiches by filling toasted buns with meat; spoon any remaining warm sauce into sandwiches. Both meat and sauce may be prepared 1 to 2 days ahead. If prepared ahead, cover cooled roast with plastic wrap or foil; refrigerate until served. To serve, reheat sauce; slice meat. Heat as directed above. Makes 6 to 8 servings.

Red-Wine Barbecue Sauce:
In a medium saucepan, heat oil. Add onion; sauté over medium heat 5 to 10 minutes or until soft. Stir in remaining ingredients. Bring to a simmer; simmer, covered, with lid ajar, about 10 minutes. Makes about 3 cups.

TIP *Tie small bunches of fresh herbs together to make a small brush for painting on butter sauces or basting sauces.*

How to Make Barbecued-Pork Sandwiches

1/Slice grilled roast into 1/4-inch thick slices. Arrange, slightly overlapping, on foil pan; brush with sauce.

2/Grill hamburger buns. Place a slice of roast on each bun half; top with remaining bun half. Pass warm barbecue sauce at the table to spoon over individual servings.

Kraut Dogs

Sausages and onions are compatible with the assertive flavor of sauerkraut.

John's Doctored Sauerkraut, page 136
8 large sausages, such as frankfurters,
   bratwurst, knockwurst, German or
   Polish sausage
8 hot dog buns

1/4 cup butter or margarine, melted
Variety of mustards, including homemade
   mustards, pages 114 and 116, if desired
Ketchup
Chopped onion, if desired

Prepare John's Doctored Sauerkraut; keep hot. Preheat grill; position a wire rack 4 to 6 inches from heat. With a sharp knife, make 2 or 3 (1/8-inch-deep) diagonal slashes in each sausage. Place sausages on rack. Turning frequently, grill 10 to 20 minutes or until browned on all sides. While sausages cook, split buns lengthwise; brush cut sides with butter or margarine. Toast buns, buttered-side down on rack, 1 to 2 minutes. If you like hot dog buns soft and steamy, like the ballpark-type, wrap in foil. Place on grill when you begin cooking; turn occasionally. Place each browned sausage in a warm bun. Spread with mustard and ketchup; top with sauerkraut and a sprinkle of chopped onion, if desired. Makes 8 servings.

Variation
South-of-the-Border Dogs: Substitute 2 cups warm canned or homemade refried beans for sauerkraut. Sprinkle grated Cheddar cheese over chopped onion.

Tangy, Sticky, Spicy Ribs

Here is a time-honored favorite, much like ribs served in popular barbecue restaurants.

2 tablespoons vegetable oil
1 onion, finely chopped
2 large garlic cloves, minced
1 cup ketchup
1/4 cup lightly packed brown sugar
1/4 cup Worcestershire sauce

1/4 cup cider vinegar
1 tablespoon chili powder
4 to 6 lbs. pork spareribs (2 racks),
 in whole slabs
Salt
Freshly ground black pepper

Preheat grill; position a wire rack 4 to 6 inches from heat. In a large saucepan, heat oil. Add onion and garlic; sauté 5 to 10 minutes or until onion is soft. Stir in ketchup, brown sugar, Worcestershire sauce, vinegar and chili powder. Bring sauce to a simmer; simmer, covered, with lid ajar, 10 minutes. Set aside. Season both sides of ribs with salt and pepper. Place ribs, meat-side up, on a rack. Cover grill; open vents slightly. Cook ribs 30 minutes; turn, cover and cook 30 minutes longer. Turn ribs, meat-side up; generously brush with sauce. Cover and cook 10 minutes longer, basting 2 or 3 times with sauce. With a sharp knife, cut grilled ribs into sections; mound on a warm platter. Pour remaining sauce into a serving dish; serve separately. Makes 4 to 6 servings.

Variations
Cocktail-Size Ribs: To serve as an appetizer, substitute smaller but very meaty baby back ribs. Cook 20 minutes on each side rather than 30 minutes; then baste with the sauce and cook 15 minutes longer as directed above.
Hickory-Smoked Ribs: Add damp hickory chips to hot coals.

Glazed Teriyaki Spareribs

Easy and tasty marinated ribs are grilled and brushed with a marmalade glaze.

1 recipe Teriyaki Marinade, page 102,
 or 1 cup bottled teriyaki sauce and marinade
4 to 6 lbs. pork spareribs (2 racks),
 in whole slabs

1/2 cup orange marmalade
Freshly ground black pepper

Prepare Teriyaki Marinade at least 1 hour ahead. Place ribs in a large baking dish. Pour marinade evenly over ribs; rub marinade into meat. Cover with plastic wrap or foil; refrigerate 3 to 4 hours or overnight, turning ribs and rubbing with marinade once or twice. Remove meat from refrigerator 30 minutes before barbecuing. Preheat grill; position a wire rack 4 to 6 inches from heat. Remove ribs from marinade; reserve marinade. Pat off excess marinade with paper towels. Place marinated ribs, meat-side down, on rack. Cover grill; open vents slightly. Turning once, cook about 1 hour or until meat is no longer pink. Meanwhile, in a small bowl, combine 1/4 cup of reserved marinade with marmalade. Turn ribs, meat-side up; brush with marmalade glaze, being careful not to drip glaze onto hot coals. Cover and cook about 10 minutes longer or until well-browned and still juicy, but no longer pink in center. Cook slightly longer if you like ribs very well-done. With a sharp knife, cut grilled ribs into sections; mound on a warm platter. Makes 4 to 6 servings.

Tangy, Sticky, Spicy Ribs; Peppery Summer Squash, page 129; Grilled Corn-in-the-Husk, page 137; and Skillet-Grilled Buttermilk Biscuits, page 148.

Barbecued Pork with Green Peppercorns

Mild-flavored green peppercorns come from a special type of pepper tree.

1 (5- to 6-lb.) pork center-cut
  loin roast
Salt
Freshly ground black pepper
1/4 cup butter or margarine,
  room temperature
1/4 cup finely chopped fresh parsley
1 tablespoon finely chopped fresh thyme
  or 1 teaspoon dried leaf thyme, crumbled

2-1/2 teaspoons drained water-packed
  green peppercorns
2 garlic cloves, minced
1/2 teaspoon salt
1 small carrot, finely chopped
1 small onion, finely chopped
1 celery stalk, finely chopped

Have butcher cut rib bones off loin roast; cut rib bones into slabs of 3 to 4 each. Season bones with salt and pepper; place bones close together on a wire rack to form a base for vegetables and loin roast to sit on. Set aside. Prepare and preheat grill for indirect cooking, page 9. In a small bowl, blend butter or margarine, parsley, thyme, peppercorns, garlic and 1/2 teaspoon salt. With a small sharp knife, make pockets between meat and layer of fat that partially covers loin. Work 3/4 of butter mixture into pockets. Tie roast at 2- to 3-inch intervals. Rub remaining butter mixture over top and sides of tied roast. Place rack with bones 4 to 6 inches over drip pan. Sprinkle carrot, onion and celery over bones. Place tied roast on vegetables. Cover grill; open vents slightly. Cook 45 minutes; turn meat. Add more briquets to maintain a constant temperature. Cook another 45 minutes or until loin has just a slight tinge of pink when cut into thickest part and registers 160F to 165F (70C to 75C) on a meat thermometer. Remove cooked pork to a carving board. Cover with foil; let stand about 10 minutes. After standing, internal temperature of pork should register 170F (77C). To carve, cut across grain into thin diagonal slices; serve on a warm platter. Makes 6 to 8 servings.

Pork Saté

Satés are slightly spicy, tender morsels of meat strung on skewers.

1/4 cup soy sauce
1/4 cup vegetable oil
1/4 cup fresh lemon juice
2 tablespoons honey

1 tablespoon curry powder
1 tablespoon chili powder
2 lbs. pork loin tenderloin,
  cut in 1-1/2-inch cubes

In a large bowl, combine soy sauce, oil, lemon juice, honey, curry powder and chili powder. Add pork; toss to coat with marinade. Cover; refrigerate 2 hours or overnight, tossing once or twice. Remove meat from refrigerator 30 minutes before barbecuing. Preheat grill; position a wire rack 4 to 6 inches from heat. Remove pork from marinade; pat off excess marinade with paper towels. Thread marinated pork cubes on long metal skewers; place skewers on rack. Grill 20 minutes or until well-browned and meat is no longer pink in center, turning frequently. Remove grilled pork cubes from skewers; serve on a warm platter. Makes 6 to 8 servings.

Variation
Add damp mesquite wood chips to hot coals for a smoky flavor.

How to Make Barbecued Pork with Green Peppercorns

1/Place bones close together on wire rack. Sprinkle vegetables over bones; set aside.

2/Make peppercorn butter. Using 3/4 of mixture, work into meat pockets. Tie roast at 2- to 3-inch intervals. Rub with remaining butter mixture; place on vegetable-topped bones.

Simple Roasted Spareribs

Inspired by the late James Beard, who loved ribs roasted and seasoned with salt and pepper. Serve with John's Doctored Sauerkraut, page 136, and boiled or steamed new potatoes.

**4 to 6 lbs. pork spareribs (2 racks),
  in whole slabs**

**Coarse salt or kosher salt
Freshly ground black pepper**

Preheat grill; position a wire rack 4 to 6 inches from heat. Place ribs, meat-side up, on rack. Generously season top with salt and pepper. Cover grill; open vents slightly. Cook ribs 30 minutes; turn ribs. Season with salt and pepper. Cover and cook 30 minutes longer or until well-browned and still juicy, but no longer pink in center. Cook 10 minutes longer if you like ribs very well-done. With a sharp knife, cut grilled ribs into sections; mound on a warm platter. Makes 4 to 6 servings.

Pork Tenderloins with Plum Sauce

Juicy pork tenderloins are done in just a few minutes, even on a small grill.

3/4 cup Chinese Plum Sauce, page 107,
   or bottled plum sauce
1/3 cup dry red wine
3 tablespoons Chinese black vinegar,
   balsamic vinegar or red-wine vinegar

1 tablespoon plus 1 teaspoon dry mustard
2 lbs. pork loin tenderloin (2 or 3 pieces)
16 to 20 pitted prunes
1 cup beef broth or bouillon

In a small bowl, combine plum sauce, red wine, vinegar and dry mustard. Place tenderloins in a large heavy food-storage bag; add plum-sauce mixture. Press out air; seal bag. Squeeze gently, pressing marinade into meat. Set bag in a large bowl; refrigerate 4 hours or overnight. Meanwhile, place prunes in a medium saucepan; pour broth or bouillon over prunes. Cover and bring to a simmer. Simmer, covered, 20 minutes or until prunes are plump and tender; keep warm. Remove meat from refrigerator 30 minutes before barbecuing. Preheat grill; position a wire rack 4 to 6 inches from heat. Remove tenderloins from marinade; pour marinade into prune mixture. Pat off excess marinade with paper towels; place marinated pork on rack. Grill 25 minutes or until meat has just a slight tinge of pink when cut into thickest part and registers 160F to 165F (70C to 75C) on a meat thermometer, turning several times so it browns evenly. While meat grills, bring prune mixture to a simmer; keep prune mixture warm. Remove cooked pork to a carving board. Cover with foil; let stand about 10 minutes. After standing, internal temperature of pork should register 170F (77C). To carve, cut across grain into thin diagonal slices; serve on a warm platter. Pour prune mixture into a serving dish; serve separately or spoon sauce over meat. Makes 6 to 8 servings.

Variation
Substitute 6 (1-inch-thick) pork loin chops for tenderloins.

Skewered Pork & Prunes

An old-fashioned combination that adapts well to grilling and is great for company.

2/3 cup unsweetened pineapple juice
1/4 cup chopped green onions
2 tablespoons soy sauce
2 tablespoons vegetable oil

1-1/2 to 1-3/4 lbs. pork loin tenderloin,
   cut in 1- to 1-1/2-inch cubes
24 pitted prunes

In a large bowl, combine pineapple juice, green onions, soy sauce and oil. Add pork and prunes; toss to coat with marinade. Cover; refrigerate 1 to 2 days, tossing occasionally. Remove meat from refrigerator 30 minutes before barbecuing. Preheat grill; position a wire rack 4 to 6 inches from heat. Remove pork and prunes from marinade; pat off excess marinade with paper towels. Carefully thread pork and prunes on long metal skewers, alternating 1 or 2 cubes of meat with each prune. Place skewers on rack. Turning frequently, grill 20 minutes or until pork is well-browned and no longer pink in center. Remove skewered meat and prunes to a warm platter. Makes 5 to 6 servings.

How to Make Honey-Spiced Glazed Ribs

1/After barbecuing ribs 1 hour, generously brush with honey sauce. Cover and cook about 20 more minutes, turning and brushing with sauce after 10 minutes.

2/With a sharp knife, cut ribs into about 3-rib sections. To serve, place ribs on a warm platter. Accompany with remaining warm honey sauce.

Honey-Spiced Glazed Ribs

Not too sweet, not too sour—just right!

**4 to 6 lbs. pork spareribs (2 racks),
  in whole slabs**
1 tablespoon cornstarch
2 tablespoons cold water
2 tablespoons vegetable oil
1 small onion, finely chopped

2/3 cup honey
1/4 cup cider vinegar
2 tablespoons Dijon-style mustard
1/2 teaspoon salt
1/4 teaspoon ground cloves
1/4 teaspoon ground allspice

Preheat grill; position a wire rack 4 to 6 inches from heat. Place ribs on rack, meat-side up. Cover grill; open vents slightly. Cook ribs 30 minutes; turn, cover and cook 30 minutes longer. Meanwhile, in a small bowl, stir cornstarch into water until smooth; set aside. Heat oil in a medium saucepan. Add onion; sauté 5 to 10 minutes until onion is soft. Stir in honey, vinegar, mustard, salt, cloves and allspice. Bring mixture to a simmer; simmer about 3 minutes. Gradually stir cornstarch mixture into onion mixture. Stirring constantly, bring to a boil; boil 1 minute. Set aside. Turn ribs, meat-side up; generously brush with honey sauce. Cover and cook about 10 minutes longer. With a sharp knife, cut grilled ribs into sections; mound on a warm platter. Pour remaining sauce into a serving dish; serve separately. Makes 4 to 6 servings.

Mixed-Sausage Grill

These are fabulous served with mustard, sauerkraut and cold beer.

**1 recipe John's Doctored Sauerkraut,
    page 136, or 1-1/2 cups other sauerkraut**
**3 lbs. mixed sausages, such as knockwurst,
    bratwurst, Italian sausage or chorizo**

**Variety of mustards, including homemade
    mustards, pages 114 and 116, if desired**
Crusty rye bread or French bread

Prepare John's Doctored Sauerkraut; keep hot. Preheat grill; position a wire rack 4 to 6 inches from heat. Meanwhile, prick sausages with a fork; place in a large saucepan. Cover with water; bring to a simmer; simmer about 10 minutes; drain. With a sharp knife, make 2 or 3 (1/8-inch-deep) diagonal slashes in each sausage. Place sausages on rack. Turning frequently, grill 10 to 20 minutes until browned on all sides. Mound on a warm platter; surround with sauerkraut. Serve with mustards and plenty of crusty rye bread or French bread. Makes 6 servings.

Smoked Leg of Pork

Good for a party because it feeds a crowd and everyone loves fresh ham. Serve with corn muffins, a Marinated Vegetable Plate, page 138 and potato salad.

**2 tablespoons coarse or kosher salt or
    1-1/2 tablespoons table salt**
1 tablespoon freshly ground black pepper
2 teaspoons dried leaf thyme, crumbled
1 teaspoon ground allspice
4 large garlic cloves, minced

1/4 cup vegetable oil
**1 (8- to 10-lb.) boneless pork
    leg roast, trimmed, tied**
**1 or 2 recipes Marge Poore's Barbecue
    Sauce, page 108**

In a small bowl, combine salt, pepper, thyme, allspice and garlic; set aside. Place pork roast in a large baking dish. Rub oil over pork; rub spice mixture over oiled pork. Cover and refrigerate 3 to 4 hours. Meanwhile, prepare Marge Poore's Barbecue Sauce; remove 1/2 to 1 cup to use as a basting sauce. Reserve remaining sauce for a table sauce. Soak hickory chips or chunks in water to cover at least 30 minutes, using 1/4 to 1/2 pound chips for a lightly smoked flavor and 3/4 to 1 pound chips for a smokier flavor. Build a charcoal fire in fire-pan of water-smoker or preheat as manufacturer directs. When coals are low-glowing and covered with a gray ash, spread out in fire-pan. Squeeze water from 1 or 2 handfuls of soaked wood chips; sprinkle on coals. Place water-pan over coals; fill with water. Position a wire rack over water-pan. Place seasoned pork on rack above water-pan; brush lightly with barbecue sauce. Cover smoker; adjust vents as manufacturer directs. Smoke 4 to 5 hours, brushing with barbecue sauce occasionally. Add more briquets and soaked wood every 45 minutes to maintain heat and smoke; add more water to water-pan, if necessary, to keep it at least 1/2 full. Cook until meat has just a slight tinge of pink when cut and a meat thermometer inserted in center of roast registers 160F to 165F (70C to 75C). Remove smoked pork to a carving board. Cover with foil; let stand about 10 minutes. After standing, internal temperature of cooked pork should reach 170F (77C). To carve, cut smoked pork across the grain into 1/4-inch-thick slices; serve on a warm platter. Pour reserved barbecue sauce into a serving dish; serve separately. Makes 12 to 18 servings.

Mixed-Sausage Grill; John's Doctored Sauerkraut, page 136; Coarse-Ground Mustard, page 114; and French Bread.

LAMB

Even though grilled lamb is popular in many parts of the world, until recently, barbecue chefs have overlooked it in favor of pork or beef. Once you've tried our Mary's Basque Lamb & Garlicky Beans, Sesame-Ginger Lamb Kabobs or Elegantly Sauced Lamb Burgers, you'll be convinced how truly wonderful lamb can be.

Years ago lamb was only available in the spring but now it is available year round. Today's lamb, compared to that sold 10 years ago, is larger and meatier with small bones and less fat in relation to the amount of meat. Technically to be labeled lamb, it must be 12 months old or less, but most lamb today is slaughtered between six and eight months.

The lamb industry has just developed new techniques of cutting up the carcass which results in a number of appealing tender cuts for the grill. They were kind enough to break down a carcass for us so we could experiment with a boneless rolled shoulder roast, a tenderloin and thick loin chops.

Along with the traditional lamb ribs and chops, leg of lamb lends itself beautifully to outdoor cooking whether it be bone-in leg of lamb, a butterflied leg or cubes for kabobs. Butterflied leg of lamb is completely boned and all visible fat is removed. It is so named because when spread flat, it resembles a butterfly. Shish kabobs, often just called kabobs, originated with Middle Eastern nomads who skewered vegetables and small pieces of meat on their swords and cooked them over an open fire.

Purchase lamb with fine-textured, rose-colored flesh surrounded by a rim of brittle, pinkish-white fat. Lamb is tender and does not have heavy marbling like beef or pork because it comes from a young animal. For this reason, lamb should be cooked only until it's pink and juicy inside and nicely browned on the outside. If cooked to the well-done stage, lamb becomes dry and flavorless. Recipes in this chapter give instructions for cooking lamb rare or medium.

Barbecued Lamb Chops

Center-cut loin lamb chops are best when served medium-rare, but can be cooked longer. Serve with Peppery Summer Squash, page 129.

4 lamb center-cut loin chops
4 bacon slices
2 garlic cloves, cut in half

1 teaspoon dried rosemary, crushed
Salt
Freshly ground black pepper

Preheat grill; position a wire rack 4 to 6 inches from heat. Wrap each chop with a bacon slice; secure with a wooden pick. Using 1/2 garlic clove for each chop, rub garlic over both sides of each chop; insert garlic between chop and bacon. Rub 1/8 teaspoon rosemary over each chop, pressing into meat; sprinkle each with salt and pepper. Place seasoned chops on rack. Cover grill, cook 5 to 7 minutes on each side for rare, 8 to 10 minutes on each side for medium and 10 to 12 minutes on each side for well-done. Remove cooked meat to a warm platter or individual plates. Makes 4 servings.

Wine-Country Lamb

A simple and delicious way to barbecue a whole leg of lamb in a covered grill.

1 cup dry red wine
1/2 cup olive oil
1/4 cup finely chopped fresh parsley
3 large garlic cloves, finely chopped
2 tablespoons finely chopped fresh
   rosemary or 1 tablespoon dried
   rosemary, crumbled

1 teaspoon salt
1/2 teaspoon freshly ground black pepper
1 (6- to 7-lb.) leg of lamb, trimmed

In a medium bowl, combine red wine, olive oil, parsley, garlic, rosemary, salt and pepper. Place lamb in a shallow roasting pan. Pour wine mixture over lamb; rub marinade into meat. Cover and refrigerate 8 hours or overnight. Turn lamb 3 or 4 times, rubbing marinade into meat with each turn. Remove meat from refrigerator 30 minutes before barbecuing. Prepare and preheat grill for indirect cooking, page 9. Position a wire rack 4 to 6 inches from heat. Remove lamb from marinade, reserving marinade; place lamb on rack directly over drip pan. Cover grill; open vents slightly. Cook 45 minutes; turn meat. Add more briquets to maintain a constant temperature. Cook 45 minutes longer or until a meat thermometer inserted in center of meat, not touching bone, registers 130F to 135F (55C) for rare or 150F to 155F (65C to 70C) for medium, brushing occasionally with reserved marinade. Remove cooked lamb to a carving board. Cover with foil; let stand about 10 minutes. After standing, internal temperature of lamb should register 140F (60C) for rare and 160F (70C) for medium. To carve, cut across grain into thin slices; serve on a warm platter. Makes 8 to 10 servings.

Spinach-Stuffed Leg of Lamb   Photo on page 57.

A bit time-consuming, but worth it—and delicious served hot, room temperature or chilled.

2 large bunches spinach, stems removed
3 tablespoons olive oil
2 large garlic cloves, finely chopped
1/2 cup fresh bread crumbs
1/4 cup raisins
1/4 cup pine nuts
1/4 cup chopped fresh basil or
   1 tablespoon dried leaf basil, crumbled

2 oz. goat cheese or cream cheese,
   room temperature
1/2 teaspoon salt
1/4 teaspoon freshly ground black pepper
1 (6- to 7-lb.) leg of lamb, boned,
   butterflied, trimmed (about 4 lbs.
   after boning and trimming)

Wash spinach to rid leaves of grit; dry with paper towels. Stack 10 to 12 spinach leaves on top of each other; roll lengthwise, jelly-roll style. Cut crosswise into 1/8-inch shreds. Repeat with remaining leaves. In a medium skillet, heat olive oil over high heat; stir in spinach and garlic. Tossing and stirring often, cook 2 minutes or until most of liquid has evaporated. Spoon spinach mixture into a medium bowl; stir in bread crumbs, raisins, pine nuts, basil, cheese, salt and pepper. Spread out lamb on a flat surface, boned-side up. Spread with spinach mixture; roll up, jelly-roll style, beginning from a long side. With heavy string, tie rolled lamb at 1-inch intervals. Prepare and preheat grill for indirect cooking, page 9. Position a wire rack 4 to 6 inches from heat. Place lamb on rack directly over drip pan. Cover grill; open vents slightly. Cook 45 minutes; turn meat. Add more briquets to maintain a constant temperature. Cook 45 minutes longer or until a meat thermometer inserted in center of meat registers 130F to 135F (55C) for rare, or 150F to 155F (65C to 70C) for medium. Remove cooked lamb to a carving board. Cover with foil; let stand about 10 minutes. After standing, internal temperature of lamb should register 140F (60C) for rare and 160F (70C) for medium. To carve, cut across grain into thin slices; serve on a warm platter. Makes 8 to 10 servings.

Simplest Charcoal-Grilled Lamb Chops

Loin chops are the tiny T-bone section of lamb, the tenderest and most expensive portion.

8 lamb loin chops, 1 inch thick
1/3 cup olive oil
Salt
Freshly ground black pepper

3 tablespoons chopped fresh rosemary or
   1 tablespoon dried rosemary, crumbled
Fresh rosemary sprigs, if desired

Rub all sides of each chop with olive oil; sprinkle with salt and pepper. Rub with chopped or crumbled rosemary. Preheat grill; position a wire rack 4 to 6 inches from heat. Drop a few rosemary sprigs directly on hot coals, if desired, so smoke billows around chops. Place seasoned chops on rack. Grill 10 to 12 minutes, turning 3 or 4 times, until well-browned on outside but still slightly pink in center. Throughout grilling, drop rosemary sprigs onto hot coals. Makes 4 servings.

How to Make Spinach-Stuffed Leg of Lamb

1/Spread boned, butterflied leg of lamb out on a flat surface. Evenly spoon spinach filling to 1/2-inch from edges. Starting with long end, roll up jelly-roll style.

2/Using heavy string, tie rolled, stuffed lamb at 1-inch intervals. After barbecuing, cut string from roast and slice across grain into thin slices.

Sesame-Ginger Lamb Kabobs

Skewered tender, lean cubes of lamb cook in minutes.

1/4 cup olive oil or vegetable oil
1/4 cup sesame oil
1/4 cup soy sauce
2 tablespoons fresh lemon juice
2 lbs. boneless lamb leg or shoulder,
   cut in 1-1/2-inch cubes

2 teaspoons grated fresh gingerroot or
   1 teaspoon ground ginger
1 teaspoon dried leaf oregano, crumbled

In a large bowl, combine olive oil or vegetable oil, sesame oil, soy sauce and lemon juice; add lamb cubes, tossing to coat. Rub marinade into lamb cubes; sprinkle ginger and oregano over top; toss again. Cover with plastic wrap or foil; refrigerate at least 1 hour or overnight, tossing lamb once or twice in marinade. Remove meat from refrigerator 30 minutes before barbecuing. Preheat grill; position a wire rack 4 to 6 inches from heat. Remove lamb cubes from marinade; pat off excess marinade with paper towels. Thread marinated lamb cubes onto long metal skewers. Place skewered lamb on rack; grill 8 to 10 minutes, turning frequently, until well-browned and cooked to desired doneness. Serve on a warm platter. Makes 6 servings.

Variation

Spread 2 cups sesame seeds on a platter. After patting off excess marinade, roll lamb cubes in sesame seeds. Thread seeded lamb cubes on skewers; grill as directed above, turning frequently. Watch carefully because seeds burn easily.

Butterflied 'n Barbecued Leg of Lamb

When boned and spread out flat, the leg cooks in 30 to 45 minutes and is a snap to carve.

1/2 cup dry red wine
1/4 cup olive oil
2 tablespoons soy sauce
2 tablespoons finely chopped fresh
   rosemary or 2 teaspoons dried
   rosemary, crumbled
Finely grated peel of 1 lemon
   (about 1-1/2 teaspoons)

2 tablespoons fresh lemon juice
1/8 to 1/4 teaspoon hot-pepper sauce
2 large garlic cloves, finely chopped
1 (6- to 7-lb.) leg of lamb, boned,
   butterflied, trimmed (about 4 lbs.
   after boning and trimming)

In a small bowl, combine red wine, olive oil, soy sauce, rosemary, lemon peel, lemon juice, hot-pepper sauce and garlic. Spread out lamb in a large roasting pan; pour marinade over lamb. Cover and refrigerate 2 to 4 hours, turning lamb once or twice. If there is not time to marinate lamb, combine marinade ingredients; brush over lamb during grilling, as directed below. If refrigerated, remove meat 30 mintues before barbecuing. Preheat grill; position a wire rack 4 to 6 inches from heat. Remove lamb from marinade, reserving marinade. Pat off excess marinade with paper towels. If desired, place lamb in an oiled wire grilling basket to help keep meat in shape and to make turning easier. Place marinated lamb on rack. Grill 30 to 45 minutes or until a meat thermometer inserted in center of meat registers 130F to 135F (55C) for rare or 150F to 155F (65C to 70C) for medium; turn frequently and brush with marinade. Remove cooked lamb to a carving board. Cover with foil; let stand about 10 minutes. After standing, internal temperature of lamb should register 140F (60C) for rare and 160F (70C) for medium. To carve, cut across grain into thin slices; serve on a warm platter. Makes 8 to 10 servings.

Grilled Lamb Burritos

An easy food to eat out of hand, without utensils, on a picnic or at the beach.

1 recipe Humus, page 127, or
   2 cups canned refried beans
1-1/2 lbs. ground lamb
1/2 cup finely chopped onion
1/2 teaspoon ground cumin
1/2 teaspoon salt

1/8 teaspoon or more hot-pepper sauce
6 (8- or 10-inch) flour tortillas
2 cups shredded iceberg lettuce
1 cup chopped green onions
2 (2-1/4-oz.) cans chopped ripe olives
1 cup dairy sour cream

Preheat grill; position a wire rack 4 to 6 inches from heat. Prepare Humus; set aside. Wrap tortillas in foil; place on edge of grill to warm. In a medium bowl, combine lamb, onion, cumin, salt and hot-pepper sauce. Shape mixture into 6 oval patties, about 5'' x 3'' and 1/2 inch thick. Place lamb patties on rack; turning frequently, grill about 10 minutes or until meat is barely pink inside. In a small saucepan, heat Humus or beans over medium heat or on grill. Place a cooked patty on one side of a warm tortilla; spread about 1/4 cup warmed Humus or beans over patty. Top with lettuce, green onions, olives and a dollop of sour cream. Fold edges of tortilla over at both ends of lamb patty; roll tortilla around filling, covering completely. Repeat with remaining tortillas, cooked patties, lettuce, green onions, olives and sour cream. Makes 6 servings.

Spinach-Stuffed Leg of Lamb, page 54; and Grilled Vegetables, page 130.

Mary's Basque Lamb & Garlicky Beans

A hearty and fragrant dinner—best on a cold winter day, followed by a brisk walk.

1 (6- to 7-lb.) leg of lamb, trimmed
3 garlic cloves, cut in quarters
2 tablespoons olive oil
2 tablespoons finely chopped fresh
   rosemary or 1 tablespoon dried
   rosemary, crumbled

Salt
Freshly ground black pepper
Garlicky Beans, see below

Garlicky Beans:
1 lb. small white beans
Water
1/2 cup butter or margarine
4 large garlic cloves, finely chopped

2 cups chopped fresh parsley
1/2 cup whipping cream
Salt
Freshly ground black pepper

Using a small sharp knife, make 12 random incisions in lamb, about 1 inch deep; insert a garlic quarter in each slit. Rub trimmed lamb with olive oil, then with rosemary; sprinkle with salt and pepper. Place seasoned lamb in a baking dish. Cover and refrigerate 4 to 6 hours or overnight. Begin preparing Garlicky Beans, setting beans to soak 1 hour. Remove meat from refrigerator 30 minutes before barbecuing. Preheat grill; position a wire rack 4 to 6 inches from heat. Place seasoned lamb on rack. Cover grill; open vents slightly. Cook 45 minutes; turn meat. Add more briquets to maintain a constant temperature. Cook 45 minutes longer or until a meat thermometer inserted in center of meat, not touching bone, registers 130F to 135F (55C) for rare or 150F to 155F (65C to 70C) for medium; turn lamb once during cooking. While lamb cooks, finish preparing Garlicky Beans. Remove cooked lamb to a carving board. Cover with foil; let stand about 10 minutes. After standing, internal temperature of lamb should register 140F (60C) for rare and 160F (70C) for medium. To carve, cut across grain into thin slices; serve on a warm platter. Meanwhile, stir a little reserved cooking liquid into beans if they are dry. Serve lamb with generous servings of warm beans. Makes 8 to 10 servings.

Garlicky Beans:
Sort and rinse beans; place in a large saucepan. Add cold water to cover. Over medium-high heat, bring water to a boil, uncovered; boil 2 minutes. Remove pan from heat. Cover; let beans soak 1 hour. Discard soaking water; rinse beans under cold running water. In same saucepan, cover beans with fresh water; bring to a simmer. Simmer about 1 hour or until beans are tender. Drain, reserving cooking liquid. In a large skillet, melt butter or margarine. Add garlic; sauté over medium heat about 2 minutes. Stir in parsley, then beans and cream. Season to taste with salt and pepper; keep warm. Makes about 6 cups.

Spit-Roasting

   With the popularity of covered grills, spit-roasting is done less and less. One advantage to spit roasting is that as the meat rotates, it bastes itself. If you build a proper fire and balance the meat on the spit, all you'll have to do is watch the time. Balancing the meat on the spit is a key factor when spit roasting. The spit **must** turn evenly or the food will cook unevenly. Holding it in your hands, turn the skewered meat on the spit to be sure you have the meat balanced.

   If you're spit-roasting in a gas or electric grill, follow your owner's manual. In a charcoal grill, build a fire about four inches longer and wider than the meat to be roasted. Place a drip-pan in front of the coals and slightly ahead of the meat. As the meat turns on the spit, the fat will roll off the front of the meat into the drip-pan.

How to Make Spit-Roasted Lamb Shoulder

1/Insert spit, lengthwise, into rolled, boneless lamb roast. For even cooking, make sure roast is evenly balanced on spit; secure tightly with tines.

2/After 45 minutes of cooking, add more briquets to maintain constant cooking temperature. Lamb should be cooked to the rare or medium stage—overcooking produces tough meat.

Spit-Roasted Lamb Shoulder

A boned-and-rolled lamb shoulder, flavored with a dry rub, is perfect for the spit.

**1 recipe Herb Rub for Lamb,
   page 110**

**1 (3-1/2- to 4-lb.) boneless lamb
   shoulder roast, rolled, tied**

Prepare Herb Rub for Lamb; rub herb mixture over surface of lamb. Cover with plastic wrap or foil; refrigerate 2 to 12 hours. Preheat grill for spit-roasting, opposite. Insert spit lengthwise into lamb, making sure meat is balanced; secure with tines. Spit-roast about 2 hours or until a meat thermometer inserted in center of meat registers 130F to 135F (55C) for rare and 150F to 155F (65C to 70C) for medium. Add more briquets after about 45 minutes to maintain a constant temperature. Remove cooked lamb to a carving board. Cover with foil; let stand about 10 minutes. After standing, internal temperature of lamb should register 140F (60C) for rare and 160F (70C) for medium. To carve, cut across grain into thin slices; serve on a warm platter. Makes 6 to 8 servings.

Rack of Lamb with Mustard-Herb Coating

An easy recipe to double if you're serving more people.

1 (about 1-1/2-lb, 8-rib) lamb
   rib rack for roasting
Salt
Freshly ground black pepper
3/4 cup fresh bread crumbs

3 tablespoons butter or margarine, melted
2 tablespoons chopped fresh parsley
1/4 cup Dijon-style mustard
2 teaspoons dried leaf tarragon, crumbled

Have butcher trim rack of lamb, removing all visible fat and the extra, thin flap of meat at one end. Also have butcher cut through chine bone. Cut and scrape meat from between long rib bones, leaving 2 to 3 inches of clean, scraped bone protruding. Cover exposed bones with a double thickness of foil to keep them from burning. Sprinkle meat with salt and pepper. Prepare and preheat grill for indirect cooking, page 9. Position a wire rack 4 to 6 inches from heat. Place lamb on rack directly over drip pan. Grill about 15 minutes, turning frequently, until browned on both sides. Meanwhile, in a small bowl, combine bread crumbs, butter or margarine and parsley; set aside. Remove cooked lamb to a platter, turning rib bones down. Spread top of lamb with mustard; sprinkle with tarragon. Press crumb mixture into mustard coating. Return lamb to grill. Cover grill; open vents slightly. Cook about 10 minutes longer. Meanwhile, preheat oven broiler for final browning of crumbs. Crumbs will not brown and become crisp on grill without overcooking lamb. Remove cooked lamb from grill to a broiler pan; broil in oven immediately or wait up to 15 minutes. Broil lamb about 4 inches from heat, 1 to 2 minutes until crumbs are well-browned. To carve, cut between ribs; mound on a warm platter. Makes 3 to 4 servings.

Lamb Saté

Serve these rosy, rare lamb strips over parslied rice. Serve with parslied rice and Grilled Onions with Mustard-Herb Butter Sauce, page 132, or Eggplant with Cilantro-Onion Butter, page 132.

1/4 cup soy sauce
1/4 cup vegetable oil
1/4 cup dry red wine or white wine
1/2 cup finely chopped green onions
2 teaspoons grated fresh gingerroot or
   1 teaspoon ground ginger

1/2 teaspoon ground cardamom
Pinch of saffron, if desired
2 lbs. lean boneless lamb leg or
   shoulder, cut in 3'' x 1'' strips,
   1/2 to 1 inch thick

In a large bowl, combine soy sauce, oil, wine, green onions, ginger, cardamom and saffron, if desired; add lamb strips, tossing to coat and rubbing marinade into lamb. Cover and refrigerate 30 minutes to 3 hours, tossing lamb once or twice in marinade. Remove meat from refrigerator 30 minutes before barbecuing. Preheat grill; position a wire rack 4 to 6 inches from heat. Remove lamb strips from marinade; pat off excess marinade with paper towels. Thread marinated lamb strips on long metal skewers, weaving in and out. Place skewered lamb on rack; grill 5 to 8 minutes, turning frequently, until well-browned and cooked to desired doneness. Removed cooked lamb to a warm platter. Makes 6 to 8 servings.

How to Make Rack of Lamb with Mustard-Herb Coating

1/Cut and scrape meat from between long rib bones, leaving 2 to 3 inches of clean scraped bone protruding.

2/Position rack 4 to 6 inches from heat. Place lamb rack directly over drip pan; grill about 15 minutes or until browned on the outside.

3/Remove lamb rack from grill; place ribs, bones down, on flat heatproof surface or a platter. Spread with mustard and tarragon. Using fingers, press crumb mixture into mustard-herb coated ribs.

4/To serve, cut between each rib; meat should be slightly pink. Arrange on a warm platter, with ribs toward center of plate. Garnish with fresh tarragon sprigs.

Orange-Mustard Lamb Skewers

The elusive flavor of this slightly sweet marinade softens any assertive lamb flavor.

1 cup orange marmalade
1/2 cup fresh orange juice
1/4 cup Dijon-style mustard
2 teaspoons Chinese five-spice powder

1/2 teaspoon salt
2 lbs. lean boneless lamb leg or shoulder,
    cut into 1-1/2-inch cubes

In a large bowl, combine marmalade, orange juice, mustard, five-spice powder and salt; add lamb cubes, tossing to coat. Rub marinade into lamb. Cover with plastic wrap or foil; refrigerate up to 2 hours. Preheat grill; position a wire rack 4 to 6 inches from heat. Remove lamb cubes from marinade; pat off excess marinade with paper towels. Thread marinated lamb cubes on long metal skewers. Place skewers on rack. Turning frequently, grill about 10 minutes for rare or 15 minutes for medium. Remove cooked lamb to a warm platter. Makes 6 to 8 servings.

Elegantly Sauced Lamb Burgers

These are entrees suitable for your most important guests.

2 lbs. ground lamb
1 teaspoon Chinese five-spice powder
2 to 3 teaspoons chopped fresh oregano or
    1 teaspoon dried leaf oregano, crumbled
1/2 teaspoon salt

1/2 teaspoon freshly ground black pepper
1 (6-oz.) pkg. blue cheese, cut into
    6 pieces
1 cup dry red wine
Red-Wine Sauce, see below

Red-Wine Sauce:
Reserved red wine marinade
1/2 cup whipping cream
1/2 cup butter or margarine,
    room temperature

Salt
Freshly ground black pepper

In a large bowl, combine lamb, five-spice powder, oregano, salt and pepper. Shape meat mixture into 6 (6'' x 4'') rectangles, each about 1/2 inch thick. Place 1/4 of cheese on one end of each rectangle; fold other end over top. Press edges to seal, making cheese-filled burgers about 4'' x 3'' and 1-1/2 inches thick. Arrange cheese-filled burgers in a single layer in a large shallow baking pan; pour red wine over top. Cover and refrigerate about 2 hours, spooning wine over top once or twice. Remove lamb burgers from wine marinade to a platter; cover and return to refrigerator. Reserve marinade for sauce. Prepare Red-Wine Sauce; set aside. Preheat grill; position a wire rack 4 to 6 inches from heat. Place chilled burgers on rack; grill 12 to 15 minutes for rare, 18 to 20 minutes for medium, turning at least once. Remove cooked burgers to a warm platter; spoon sauce over top. Makes 6 servings.

Red-Wine Sauce:
Pour red-wine marinade into a medium saucepan; boil until reduced to 1/4 cup. Stir in cream; boil about 2 minutes until sauce reduces slightly. Remove from heat. Whisk in butter or margarine, 2 tablespoons at a time, until each addition is absorbed into sauce. Season to taste with salt and pepper. To serve, gently reheat sauce, if necessary. Makes about 1 cup.

Orange-Mustard Lamb Skewers; and Rice Salad with Mustard Vinaigrette, page 146.

Lamb Riblets with Tomato-Mint Sauce

Lamb riblets, cut from the breast section, are only about 3 inches long.

1/2 cup red-wine vinegar
1/3 cup sugar
1 cup chopped fresh mint leaves or
   2 tablespoons dried leaf mint, crumbled

1 (8-oz.) can tomato sauce
3 to 3-1/2 lbs. lamb riblets
Salt
Freshly ground black pepper

In a small saucepan, combine vinegar and sugar; bring to a boil. Boil only until sugar dissolves. Remove pan from heat; stir in mint and tomato sauce. Preheat grill; position a wire rack 4 to 6 inches from heat. Season ribs generously with salt and pepper. Place seasoned ribs on rack; grill about 20 minutes, turning occasionally. After 20 minutes, turn ribs frequently, brushing with sauce after every turn. Grill a total of about 35 minutes or to desired doneness. Serve immediately or pour into a container with a tight-fitting lid; refrigerate up to 3 days. Makes 4 servings.

Smoked Leg of Lamb

A mild, woodsy smoke flavors the lamb nicely in a water-smoker.

Piquant Mint Sauce, see below
1 recipe Dry Rub for Lamb, page 110

2 tablespoons vegetable oil
1 (6- to 7-lb.) leg of lamb, trimmed

Piquant Mint Sauce:
1/2 cup white-wine vinegar or cider vinegar
1/4 cup sugar

1/2 cup chopped fresh mint leaves

Prepare Piquant Mint Sauce; set aside. Prepare Dry Rub for Pork or Lamb; set aside. Rub oil over lamb; rub with dry rub. Place seasoned lamb in a shallow dish. Cover and refrigerate 3 to 12 hours. Soak apple, alder or other mild wood chips in water to cover at least 30 minutes, using 1/4 to 1/2 pound wood chips for a lightly smoked flavor and 3/4 to 1 pound wood chips for a smokier flavor. Build a charcoal fire in fire-pan of water-smoker or preheat as manufacturer directs. When coals are low-glowing and covered with a gray ash, spread out in fire-pan. Squeeze water from soaked wood chips; sprinkle over coals. Place water-pan over coals; fill with water. Position a wire rack over water-pan; place seasoned lamb on rack above water pan. Cover smoker; adjust vents as manufacturer directs. Smoke lamb about 2-1/2 hours. Add more briquets and soaked wood every 45 minutes to maintain heat and smoke; add more water to water-pan, if necessary, to keep it at least 1/2 full. Cook until a meat thermometer inserted in meat, not touching bone, registers 130F to 135F (55C) for rare or 150F to 155F (65C to 70C) for medium. Remove cooked lamb to a carving board. Cover with foil; let stand about 10 minutes. After standing, internal temperature of lamb should register 140F (60C) for rare and 160F (70C) for medium. Serve hot or cool to room temperature. To carve, cut across grain into thin slices; serve on a warm platter. Serve with mint sauce. Makes 8 to 10 servings.

Piquant Mint Sauce:
In a small saucepan, combine vinegar and sugar; bring to a boil. Boil only until sugar dissolves. Remove pan from heat; stir in mint. Pour into a small serving dish; let stand at least 1 hour at room temperature to let flavors blend or refrigerate up to 24 hours. Pour into a serving dish. Makes about 2/3 cup.

POULTRY

The backyard chef can choose from a wide variety of poultry, including diminutive squab and plump turkey. All varieties produce spectacular results on the grill. Chicken is an all-time favorite for barbecuing. Its mild, delicate flavor suits nearly any seasoning or sauce—tomato-rich, tangy All-American Barbecue Sauce or subtle citrus bouquet in Lemon-Roasted Chicken. There are about as many ways to cook chicken on the grill as there are barbecuers, because chicken is compatible with so many seasonings.

If poultry is frozen, leave the original wrapping on and thaw in the refrigerator, allowing 24 hours for each 5 pounds. To quick-thaw, cover the bird with cold water and allow 1/2 hour per pound, changing the water about every 1/2 hour.

Exotic game birds, such as quail and squab, are ideal for butterflying, marinating and grilling. Don't limit your enjoyment of goose and turkey to the holiday season. This duo, grilled, barbecued or smoke-cooked, will add a festive note to an outdoor meal in any season. In a water smoker, turkey is steam-cooked by using a flavored liquid in the water-pan and/or water-soaked aromatic wood chips among the coals, giving it an irresistible smoky flavor.

Marinating poultry in an oil-based marinade or brushing it with melted butter helps keep it from sticking to the rack and seals in natural juices. Brush or baste poultry lightly and carefully with oil-based marinades and butter sauces to avoid flare-ups. Keep a spray bottle of water nearby to douse any flames.

Cook poultry slowly at an even temperature, 4 to 6 inches from the heat; otherwise, the outside will char and the inside won't be cooked. If you have time, bring the poultry to room temperature before grilling to ensure even cooking. The exception to slow-cooking is quail and squab, which should be grilled quickly about 4 inches from the heat.

Use the following guidelines for perfectly cooked poultry. Whole, halved or quartered chicken or turkey is done when a rapid-response thermometer inserted between the thigh and breast registers 180F to 185F (80C to 85C), or juices run clear. Drumsticks and leg joints will move easily and breast meat will have a tinge of pink when slashed to the bone. Squab, duck, pheasant and Cornish game hens should be cooked only to 165F to 170F (75C) or they will be dry.

For maximum flavor and juiciness, cover whole grilled poultry with foil and let stand 5 to 20 minutes before carving. If well-covered with foil and a clean towel, turkey can stand up to 1-1/2 hours. This allows the juices to settle and prevents excess loss of moisture as you carve the bird.

Roasted Chicken with Backyard Vegetables

An old-fashioned Sunday dinner on the barbecue that smells heavenly while roasting.

1 (5- to 6-lb.) roasting chicken,
   giblets and neck removed
6 fresh fennel sprigs, if desired
6 fresh rosemary sprigs, if desired
2 tablespoons butter or margarine,
   room temperature
2 tablespoons chopped fresh fennel or
   2 teaspoons dried leaf tarragon,
   crumbled
Salt
Freshly ground black pepper

12 shallots or boiling onions or
   white parts of 12 green onions
6 medium carrots, cut in 2-inch pieces
4 to 6 whole garlic bulbs, unpeeled
1/3 cup olive oil
1/4 cup butter or margarine, melted
1/2 cup dry white wine
2 tablespoons chopped fresh parsley
Fresh watercress sprigs
Crusty French bread

Preheat grill; position a wire rack 4 to 6 inches from heat. Rinse chicken; pat dry with paper towels. Fill cavity of chicken with fennel and rosemary sprigs, if desired. In a small bowl, combine 2 tablespoons butter or margarine and chopped fennel or tarragon; set aside. Starting at neck, gently slide your fingers under skin covering breast, gradually working between flesh and skin down toward thighs. Work herbed butter under skin, covering all breast meat. Season chicken inside and out with salt and pepper. Fold wing tips behind shoulder joints and under bird. Truss with heavy string, page 77. Place trussed chicken, breast-side up, in a large roasting pan fitted with a wire rack. Surround with shallots or onions, carrots and garlic. Drizzle olive oil over vegetables, being sure garlic is completely covered; set roasting pan on rack. Cover grill; open vents slightly. After 30 minutes, stir vegetables; baste chicken with 1/4 cup melted butter or margarine. Pour wine over chicken and vegetables. Cover and roast 30 minutes longer, basting chicken with juices from pan. Add more briquets after about 45 minutes to maintain a constant temperature. Cover and cook 30 minutes longer or until a meat thermometer inserted in inner-thigh muscle registers 180F to 185F (80C to 85C) or until juices run clear when a knife is inserted between thigh and breast. Vegetables should be tender when pierced with a knife. Remove cooked chicken to a carving board. Cover with foil; let stand about 10 minutes. Leave vegetables in pan in covered grill with vents closed to keep warm. Carve chicken; place chicken pieces on center of a warm platter. Arrange warm vegetables around chicken; sprinkle with parsley. Garnish platter with watercress. Pour pan juices into a small serving dish. Garlic is now as soft and sweet as butter. Separate garlic cloves with your fingers, squeezing to press out garlic. Spread soft garlic on crusty French bread. Makes 6 servings.

How to Make a Foil Grill Cover

If your grill has no cover, you can still cook roasts, poultry and fish that should be covered.

Clip off the hooks of six to eight wire coat hangers; straighten the wires. By twisting two or three wires together, form a circle that fits on the rack just inside the grill.

With the remaining wires, construct an umbrella-shaped frame, using the circle as the base. Fasten the ends of the umbrella wires to the circle base. You may need to use some lightweight wire to help hold these together.

Cover the umbrella frame with heavy foil, leaving the foil open at the top of the dome, as a vent for temperature control. This idea can be adapted to rectangular and square grills.

How to Make Roasted Chicken with Backyard Vegetables

1/Starting at neck, gently slide your fingers under skin over breast. Gently work fingers between flesh and skin, down toward thighs. This creates a pouch for herb butter.

2/Place a generous amount of herb butter in a tablespoon. Place spoon under skin over breast; using your fingers, press skin into bowl of spoon to remove butter. Remove spoon. Press fingers on skin to evenly spread butter over breast.

Chicken Breasts au Citron

A good barbecued chicken for dieters or those who like white meat only.

1 cup unsweetened pineapple juice
3/4 cup fresh orange juice
2 tablespoons finely grated lemon peel
1/2 cup fresh lemon juice
3 garlic cloves, minced
1 tablespoon chopped fresh thyme or
  1 teaspoon dried leaf thyme, crumbled

1/2 teaspoon salt
1/4 teaspoon freshly ground black pepper
12 small chicken-breast halves
  (about 5 lbs. total)

In a medium bowl, combine pineapple juice, orange juice, lemon peel, lemon juice, garlic, thyme, salt and pepper; set aside. Rinse chicken; pat dry with paper towels. Place 6 rinsed chicken-breast halves in each of 2 large heavy food-storage bags. Pour 1/2 of juice marinade into each bag. Press out air; seal bags. Squeeze gently, rubbing marinade into chicken. Place each bag in a large bowl; refrigerate 2 to 4 hours, turning and rubbing marinade into chicken several times. Remove chicken from refrigerator 30 minutes before barbecuing. Preheat grill; position a wire rack 4 to 6 inches from heat. Remove breasts from marinade; place on rack. Grill about 25 minutes, turning frequently, until well-browned on both sides. Do not overcook. Remove cooked chicken to a warm platter. Makes 6 servings.

All-American Chicken with Tangy Sauce

This is just like the tangy chicken served in barbecue restaurants.

1 recipe All-American Barbecue Sauce, page 101	**Salt**
5 to 6 lbs. assorted frying-chicken pieces	**Freshly ground black pepper**
1/4 cup vegetable oil	**Watercress sprigs or parsley sprigs**

Prepare All-American Barbecue Sauce; set aside. Preheat grill; position a wire rack 4 to 6 inches from heat. Rinse chicken pieces; pat dry with paper towels. Rub chicken pieces lightly with oil; season with salt and pepper. Place seasoned chicken, skin-side down, on rack. If you are using both dark and light-meat, place dark meat on grill 15 minutes before breasts or wing pieces; white meat cooks faster than dark meat pieces. Grill 10 to 15 minutes. Turn chicken; grill about 10 minutes longer. When well-browned on both sides, brush lightly with barbecue sauce. Grill about 10 minutes longer, turning frequently and brushing with sauce after each turn. Chicken is done when meat is no longer pink when slashed in thickest portion. Remove cooked chicken to a platter; garnish with watercress or parsley. Pour remaining sauce into a small serving dish; serve separately. Makes 6 to 8 servings.

Grilled Paillard with Cilantro-Yogurt Sauce

Paillard is a boneless, pounded chicken breast that grills very quickly.

Cilantro-Yogurt Sauce, see below	**1/2 teaspoon salt**
8 boneless chicken-breast halves, skinned	**1/4 teaspoon freshly ground black pepper**
1/2 cup olive oil	**8 lime wedges**
2 tablespoons fresh lemon juice	
2 to 3 teaspoons finely chopped fresh tarragon or 1 teaspoon dried leaf tarragon, crumbled	

Cilantro-Yogurt Sauce:

8 oz. plain yogurt (1 cup)	**2 to 3 tablespoons finely chopped mint**
2 to 3 tablespoons minced cilantro	**1/2 teaspoon ground cumin**

Prepare Cilantro-Yogurt Sauce; set aside. Rinse chicken; pat dry with paper towels. Place rinsed chicken breasts, 1 at a time, between 2 pieces of plastic wrap. Pound with flat side of a meat mallet until breast is 1/4 inch thick throughout. Arrange pounded chicken breasts, in a single layer, in a large flat baking dish. In a medium bowl, whisk together olive oil, lemon juice, tarragon, salt and pepper; pour over chicken. Turn chicken to coat both sides; cover with plastic wrap or foil. Refrigerate at least 2 hours or overnight. Remove chicken from refrigerator 30 minutes before barbecuing. Preheat grill; position a wire rack 4 to 6 inches from heat. Remove chicken from marinade, reserving marinade. Do not pat off excess marinade. Place marinated chicken on rack. Grill about 6 minutes turning chicken and brushing with reserved marinade every 2 minutes. *Do not overcook.* Chicken is done when meat is slightly pink when slashed. Place chicken on a warm platter; place a small spoonful of Cilantro-Yogurt Sauce on each piece. Arrange lime wedges around edge of platter. Pour remaining sauce into a serving bowl; serve separately. Makes 4 to 8 servings.

Cilantro-Yogurt Sauce:
In a small bowl, combine yogurt, cilantro, mint and cumin. Makes about 1 cup.

All-American Chicken with Tangy Sauce; Fresh-Corn Salad, page 145; Old-Fashioned Potato Salad, page 142; and Red, White & Blue Tart, page 156.

H-E Ranch Barbecued Chicken

We first had this grilled over grape twigs and dry oak—simple, yet exceptionally delicious.

1/2 cup butter or margarine
1/2 cup fresh lemon juice
1/4 cup chopped fresh tarragon or
　1 tablespoon dried leaf tarragon,
　crumbled

2 (2-1/2- to 3-lb.) broiler-fryer
　chickens, cut in half
Fresh rosemary sprigs, if desired

Preheat grill; position a wire rack 4 to 6 inches from heat. In a small pan, melt butter or margarine over low heat; stir in lemon juice and tarragon. Keep butter sauce warm over very low heat; pan may be set on edge of grill. Rinse chicken; pat dry with paper towels. Place rinsed chicken on rack, skin-side up. Grill about 12 minutes until well-browned; turn chicken. Drop a few rosemary sprigs directly on hot coals, if desired, so smoke billows around chicken. Throughout grilling, drop rosemary sprigs onto hot coals. Being careful that butter doesn't drip onto coals, spoon butter sauce over chicken, letting sauce settle into bony crevices. Cook 5 minutes; baste again with butter sauce. Cook 5 to 10 minutes longer or until a meat thermometer inserted in inner-thigh muscle registers 180F to 185F (80C to 85C) or until juices run clear when a knife is inserted between thigh and breast. Remove cooked chicken to a warm platter. Makes 4 to 8 servings.

Spit-Roasted Turkey

To be well-balanced and cook evenly, turkey weight should not exceed 12 pounds.

1 recipe Herb-Butter Baste from Smoked
　Turkey with Herb-Butter Baste,
　page 81
1 (10- to 12-lb.) turkey, thawed if
　frozen, giblets and neck removed

Salt
Freshly ground black pepper

Prepare Herb-Butter Baste; set aside. Preheat grill as directed for spit-roasting, page 58. Rinse turkey; pat dry with paper towels. **Do not stuff a turkey to be spit-roasted.** Season turkey inside and out with salt and pepper. If marinating turkey, read page 100 and choose from marinades starting on page 102. Secure drumsticks under band of skin near tail or in metal clip that comes with turkey. Fasten neck skin over neck opening with metal skewers. Tie heavy string around breast to hold wings flat. Insert spit rod into turkey just below breast bone; bring out through tucked-in tail and under secured drumsticks. Fasten tines firmly, at right angles to each other, into each end of turkey. Make sure turkey is centered and balanced evenly as rotisserie rotates. Brush turkey with Herb-Butter Baste; continue basting throughout cooking. Add more briquets after about 45 minutes to maintain a constant temperature. Spit-roast 25 to 35 minutes per pound or until a meat thermometer inserted in inner-thigh muscle registers 180F to 185F (80C to 85C) or until juices run clear when a knife is inserted between thigh and breast. Remove cooked turkey to a carving board. Cover with foil; let stand about 10 minutes. Carve turkey; place pieces on a warm platter. Makes 10 to 12 servings.

TIP *Bring poultry almost to room temperature before grilling. This allows for faster, more even cooking.*

How to Make Chicken Griswold

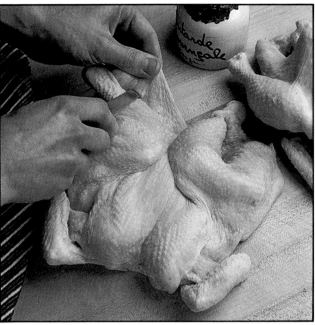

1/Place chicken on a flat surface, neck-side down, with back facing you. Using a sharp knife, cut lengthwise from tail to neck down backbone.

2/Strike breastbone firmly with your fist to break ridge of backbone and flatten breast. Make a small cut in skin on both sides of chicken between thigh and tip of breast. Push leg bones through slits.

Chicken Griswold

This quick-to-make chicken is spicy hot, and low in calories.

**2 (2-1/2- to 3-lb.) broiler-fryer
  chickens, giblets and necks removed**

**2/3 cup Dijon-style mustard
1 to 2 tablespoons red (cayenne) pepper**

Preheat grill; position a wire rack 4 to 6 inches from heat. Rinse chickens; pat dry with paper towels. Set a chicken on a flat surface, back of bird facing you, neck down. With a sharp knife, cut chicken lengthwise down backbone, slitting from tail to neck. Lay chicken flat, skin-side up. Strike breastbone firmly with your fist to bend or break ridge of bone and flatten breast. With a small pointed knife, make a small cut in skin on both sides of chicken between thigh and tip of breast. Push leg bones through slits. Repeat with remaining chicken. Using 1/2 of mustard, rub over skin of chickens; dust each with red pepper. The more red pepper you use, the spicier the flavor. Place seasoned chickens on rack, skin-side down. Grill 15 minutes; turn chickens. Spread remaining mustard over skin; sprinkle with remaining red pepper, if desired. Grill 5 minutes longer. Cover grill; open vents slightly. Cook 10 minutes longer. Remove cover; grill 5 minutes longer, turning once or twice so chickens are evenly browned on all sides. Some of mustard coating may stick to rack or fall through rack onto coals. Chicken is done when a meat thermometer inserted in inner-thigh muscle registers 180F to 185F (80C to 85C) or until juices run clear when a knife is inserted between thigh and breast. Remove cooked chicken to a warm platter. Makes 4 to 8 servings.

Butterflied Squab

Squab is a domesticated pigeon and has dark, richly flavored meat.

2 cups dry red wine
1/2 cup olive oil
1 teaspoon fennel seeds
1 teaspoon juniper berries
1/2 teaspoon salt
1/2 teaspoon freshly ground black pepper

1-1/2 teaspoons finely chopped fresh
   thyme or 1/2 teaspoon dried leaf
   thyme, crumbled
6 squab (about 6 lbs. total)
Watercress sprigs

In a medium bowl, combine wine, olive oil, fennel seeds, juniper berries, salt, pepper and thyme; set aside. Rinse squab; pat dry with paper towels. Set a squab on a flat surface, back of bird facing you, neck down. With a sharp knife, cut squab lengthwise down backbone, slitting from tail to neck. Lay squab flat, skin-side up. Strike breastbone firmly with your fist to bend or break ridge of bone and flatten breast. Repeat with remaining squab. Place 3 butterflied squab in each of 2 large heavy food-storage bags. Pour 1/2 of wine mixture into each bag. Press out air; seal bags. Squeeze gently, rubbing marinade into squab. Place each bag into a large bowl; refrigerate at least 4 hours or overnight, turning and rubbing marinade into squab several times. Remove squab from refrigerator 30 minutes before barbecuing. Preheat grill; position a wire rack 4 to 6 inches from heat. Remove squab from marinade, reserving marinade; pat off excess marinade with paper towels. Place marinated squab on rack. Grill 15 to 20 minutes, turning and brushing with reserved marinade 3 or 4 times. Squabs are done when well-browned and breast meat is slightly pink when slashed to bone in thickest portion. Remove cooked squab to a warm platter; garnish with watercress sprigs. Makes 6 servings.

Variations

Substitute 6 butterflied poussin (very young) chickens for squab. Prepare as directed above; grill about 7 minutes on each side, until lightly browned. Turn skin-side up. Cover barbecue; grill about 20 minutes longer.

Skewered Livers with Ham & Mushrooms

These make good appetizers or a first course before the main barbecue.

3 tablespoons olive oil
1 tablespoon soy sauce
1/4 cup chopped green onions with tops
1/4 teaspoon dried leaf thyme
1/4 teaspoon freshly ground black pepper
1-1/2 lbs. chicken livers, trimmed and halved

8 oz. cooked ham, 1/2 inch thick,
   cut in 1-inch squares
18 large mushroom, stems removed
6 tablespoons butter or margarine,
   melted, or 1/3 cup olive oil

In a medium bowl, combine 3 tablespoons olive oil, soy sauce, green onions, thyme and pepper. Add livers; toss to coat. Cover with plastic wrap or foil; refrigerate at least 1 hour, tossing once or twice. Preheat grill; position a wire rack 4 to 6 inches from heat. Thread marinated livers, ham pieces and mushroom caps on 6 skewers, beginning and ending each skewer with a mushroom cap. Brush skewered ingredients with butter, margarine or olive oil. Place skewers on rack. Grill 8 to 12 minutes, turning occasionally and brushing each time with butter, margarine or olive oil. *Do not overcook.* Livers should be browned outside and slightly pink when slashed in thickest portion. Remove cooked livers to a warm platter. Makes 6 servings.

Roasted Game Hens with Garlic Butter

Photo on cover.

Roasted game hens tend to be dry, but this butter will help keep them moist and flavorful.

2 shallots or white part of
   2 green onions, finely chopped
8 large garlic cloves, finely chopped
1/2 cup butter or margarine,
   room temperature
2 tablespoons finely chopped fresh
   tarragon or 2 teaspoons dried leaf
   tarragon, crumbled

2 tablespoons finely chopped fresh parsley
1/2 teaspoon salt
1/4 teaspoon freshly ground black pepper
4 Cornish game hens, thawed if frozen,
   giblets and necks removed (24 oz. each)
Parsley sprigs

In a small bowl, combine shallots or green onions, garlic, butter or margarine, tarragon, chopped parsley, salt and pepper. Or, in a food processor fitted with a metal blade, combine whole peeled shallots or white part of green onions, garlic cloves, butter or margarine and seasonings. Process with on/off motions 30 to 45 seconds until mixture forms a paste; set aside. Preheat grill; position a wire rack 4 to 6 inches from heat. Rinse hens; pat dry with paper towels. Starting at neck, gently slide your fingers under skin covering breast, gradually working between flesh and skin down toward thighs. Proceed gently so you don't tear skin. Evenly divide butter mixture in 4 portions; spoon under skin of each bird. Work herbed butter under skin, covering all breast meat. Insert a few parsley sprigs into each body cavity. Fold wing tips behind shoulder joints and under birds; truss with heavy string, page 77. Place birds on rack, breast-side down. Grill about 20 minutes, turning every 5 minutes, until lightly browned on all sides. Turn breast-side up; cover grill. Cook 20 to 25 minutes longer. Birds are done when meat is no longer pink when knife is inserted between thigh and breast and juices run clear. Remove cooked game hens to a warm platter. Makes 4 servings.

Quail with Mustard & Tarragon

These small birds don't need much cooking. Grill them quickly and close to the heat.

1/2 cup Dijon-style mustard
1/2 cup dry red wine
1 to 2 tablespoons finely chopped fresh
   tarragon or 2 teaspoons dried leaf
   tarragon, crumbled

8 quail (2 to 3 lbs. total)

In a medium bowl, combine mustard, red wine and tarragon; set aside. Rinse quail; pat dry with paper towels. Set a rinsed quail on a flat surface, back of bird facing you, neck down. With a sharp knife, cut each quail lengthwise down backbone, slitting from tail to neck. Lay quail flat, skin-side up. Strike breastbone firmly with your fist to bend or break ridge of bone and flatten breast. Repeat with remaining quail. Place split quail in a large heavy food-storage bag. Add marinade; press out air and seal bag. Squeeze gently, rubbing marinade into quail. Place bag in a large bowl; refrigerate at least 2 hours or overnight, turning and rubbing marinade into quail several times. Remove quail from refrigerator 30 minutes before barbecuing. Preheat grill; position a wire rack 4 to 6 inches from heat. Remove quail from marinade; pat off excess marinade with paper towels. Place marinated quail on rack. Grill 12 to 15 minutes, turning every 3 minutes, until browned on all sides. Quail are done when breast meat is slightly pink when slashed to bone in thickest portion. Remove cooked quail to a warm platter. Makes 4 servings.

Herbranson's Roasted Stuffed Turkey

This succulent, golden bird with a savory stuffing can be prepared in any covered grill.

1 lb. bulk pork sausage
1/4 cup butter or margarine
1 onion, finely chopped
1 cup finely chopped celery
2 garlic cloves, minced
2 cooking apples, peeled, finely chopped
2 teaspoons finely grated lemon peel
7 cups fresh white bread crumbs
   (about 1 lb.)

Salt
Freshly ground black pepper
1 (12- to 14-lb.) turkey, thawed if frozen,
   giblets and neck removed
8 tablespoons butter or margarine, room
   temperature
Turkey Gravy, see below

Turkey Gravy:
3 tablespoons butter or margarine
3 tablespoons all-purpose flour
2 cups hot chicken or turkey stock or milk

Salt
Freshly ground black pepper

In a large skillet, brown sausage until no longer pink, breaking apart with a fork. With a slotted spoon, transfer cooked sausage to a large bowl. Discard drippings from skillet. In same skillet, melt 1/4 cup butter or margarine. Add onion, celery and garlic; sauté 5 to 10 minutes or until vegetables are soft and translucent. Add to cooked sausage; add apples, lemon juice and bread crumbs. Toss to distribute; season with salt and pepper. Set aside. Pull fat from tail and neck of turkey. Rinse turkey; pat dry with paper towels. Sprinkle cavity with salt and pepper. Loosely spoon stuffing into cavity until about 3/4 full. Do not pack tightly; dressing will expand during cooking. Spoon any extra stuffing into a small fireproof casserole. Cover with lid or foil; place on rack next to turkey during last 40 minutes of cooking, or heat in oven until warmed through. Fold wing tips behind shoulder joints and under bird. Truss turkey with heavy string, page 77. Prepare and preheat grill for indirect cooking, page 9; position a wire rack 4 to 6 inches from heat. Place turkey, breast-side up, on rack above drip pan. Cover grill; open vents fully. Cook 20 minutes. Protecting your fingers with a folded paper towel, rub legs and breast of turkey with 2 tablespoons room temperature butter or margarine. Repeat rubbing with butter or margarine every 30 minutes. Add more briquets after about 45 minutes to maintain a constant temperature. Cook turkey a total of 2 hours or until a meat thermometer inserted in inner-thigh muscle registers 180F to 185F (80C to 85C) or until juices run clear when a knife is inserted between thigh and breast. Remove cooked turkey to a carving board. Cover with foil; let stand at least 20 minutes or cover foil with a clean towel and let stand up to 1-1/2 hours. After standing, turkey will still be warm enough to serve. While turkey stands, pour drippings into a glass measuring cup or glass bowl. When fat rises to top, spoon off and discard all but about 3 tablespoons fat. Prepare Turkey Gravy just before serving; keep warm. Spoon dressing from turkey into a serving dish. To carve turkey, cut turkey breast across grain into thin slices; slice meat from wings and legs. Serve carved turkey with gravy and dressing. Makes about 12 to 14 servings.

Turkey Gravy:

Melt butter or margarine in a medium saucepan over medium heat. Stir in flour; cook about 2 minutes, stirring constantly. Gradually whisk in stock or milk. Stirring constantly, bring to a simmer; simmer 5 minutes or until slightly thickened. Stir in reserved drippings; bring back to a simmer. Season with salt and pepper. Pour gravy into a warm serving bowl. Makes 3 to 4 cups.

Herbranson's Roasted Stuffed Turkey; Marinated Vegetable Plate, page 138; and your favorite cranberry relish.

Buffalo Wings

These marinated chicken wings make a popular finger food to serve with dipping sauces.

1 cup cider or red-wine vinegar
1 tablespoon chili powder
1 teaspoon salt
1 teaspoon freshly ground black pepper
2 teaspoons vegetable oil

2 teaspoons Worcestershire sauce
1 to 2 teaspoons hot-pepper sauce
3 lbs. chicken wings (15 to 18 wings)
Red-Chili Sauce or Blue-Cheese Sauce,
    page 112

In a small bowl, combine vinegar, chili powder, salt, pepper, oil, Worcestershire sauce and hot-pepper sauce. Rinse wings; pat dry with paper towels. Place chicken wings in a large food-storage bag; add marinade. Press out air; seal bag. Squeeze gently, pressing marinade into meat. Set bag in a large bowl; let stand 30 minutes at room temperature or overnight in refrigerator. If refrigerated overnight, remove from refrigerator 30 minutes before barbecuing. Preheat grill; position a wire rack 4 to 6 inches from heat. Remove chicken wings from marinade; arrange in a single layer on rack. Cook in an open or covered grill 30 to 40 minutes or until skins are crisp and golden brown, turning frequently and basting with marinade, if desired. Remove cooked wings to a warm platter. Serve with Red-Chili Sauce or Blue-Cheese Sauce. Makes 4 appetizer servings or 2 main-dish servings.

Rolled Turkey Breast

Have your butcher bone and butterfly the turkey breast.

1 (6-lb.) turkey breast, boned,
    butterflied, skin on
1 tablespoon butter or margarine
1 medium onion, finely chopped
8 oz. bulk pork sausage
1-1/2 cups cooked long grain white rice
1/4 cup currants
1/4 cup slivered almonds

1/4 cup pine nuts
2 tablespoons chopped fresh parsley
1/2 teaspoon ground cinnamon
1/4 teaspoon ground cloves
Salt
Freshly ground black pepper
1/4 cup Dijon-style mustard
Parsley sprigs

Preheat grill, position a wire rack 4 to 6 inches from heat. Lay turkey breast, skin-side down, between 2 layers of plastic wrap. Pound with flat side of a meat mallet until 3/4 inch thick throughout, making turkey breast measure about 16'' x 11''. In a large cast-iron skillet, on rack, melt butter or margarine. Add onion; sauté 5 to 10 minutes or until soft. Add sausage; cook until no pink remains, breaking up meat with a fork. Stir in rice, currants, almonds, pine nuts, parsley, cinnamon, cloves, salt and pepper. Taste and adjust seasonings. Set aside to cool. Spread mustard evenly over turkey breast. Spoon stuffing over mustard to within 1/2 inch of all edges. Use plastic wrap to lift and tightly roll turkey breast, jelly-roll style, starting from a short side. Tie rolled, stuffed breast with heavy string in 2 or 3 places lengthwise and crosswise so finished roll is tightly secured and resembles a sausage. Rub salt and pepper onto turkey skin. Place turkey roll on rack; cover grill. Cook 1 hour and 15 minutes to 1 hour and 30 minutes or until a meat thermometer inserted in center of meat registers 180F to 185F (80C to 85C) or until juices run clear when meat is slashed with a knife. Turn turkey frequently to brown evenly; if turkey is browning too quickly, move hot coals directly under roll to side of grill. Add more briquets after about 45 minutes to maintain a constant temperature. Remove cooked turkey to a carving board. Cover with foil; let stand about 10 minutes. To carve, cut and discard string. Cut turkey into 1/2-inch-thick slices. arrange on a warm platter. Garnish with parsley sprigs. Makes about 8 servings.

How to Make Lemon-Roasted Chicken

1/To release oil essence from lemons, soften lemons by rolling firmly between palm of hand and countertop. Prick each lemon 15 to 20 times with skewer or knife point; place both lemons in chicken cavity.

2/To truss, bend wing tips under body. Using 2 lengths of heavy string, tie wings to body. With 2 more lengths of string, tie upper legs/thighs to body. Bring legs together and tie securely with another length of string.

Lemon-Roasted Chicken

This slow-cooked chicken is moist and lightly perfumed with lemon and tarragon.

**1 (5- to 6-lb.) roasting chicken,
  giblets and neck removed**
Salt
Freshly ground black pepper
2 lemons

**5 or 6 fresh tarragon, rosemary,
  sage or parsley sprigs**
1/4 cup butter or margarine
1 tablespoon fresh lemon juice

Preheat grill; position a wire rack 4 to 6 inches from heat. In a small saucepan, melt butter or margarine. Remove pan from heat; stir in lemon juice. Set aside; keep warm. Rinse chicken; pat dry with paper towels. Season inside and out with salt and pepper. Soften lemons by rolling firmly between palm of one hand and countertop. Prick lemon peel 15 to 20 times with a skewer or knife point. Place pricked lemons in chicken cavity; add fresh herb sprigs. Pull skin over cavity opening. Truss legs with heavy string; see photos above. Place chicken, breast-side down, on rack. Cover grill; open vents slightly. Grill 25 minutes; turn chicken breast-side up. Baste with butter sauce; cover and cook 30 minutes longer. Baste again; add more briquets to maintain a constant temperature. Cover and cook about 30 minutes longer or until a meat thermometer inserted in inner-thigh muscle registers 180F to 185F (80C to 85C) or until juices run clear when a knife is inserted between thigh and breast. Remove cooked chicken to a carving board. Cover with foil; let stand about 10 minutes. Carve chicken; place chicken pieces on a warm platter. Makes 6 servings.

Gayle Wilson's French-Style Chicken

Chicken pieces are marinated in a zippy vinaigrette.

3 tablespoons red-wine vinegar
1 tablespoon Dijon-style mustard
1 large garlic clove, minced
1 large shallot, minced

1 teaspoon salt
2 teaspoons freshly ground black pepper
3/4 cup olive oil
About 4 lbs. assorted frying-chicken pieces

In a small bowl, whisk together vinegar, mustard, garlic, shallot, salt and pepper; continue whisking while slowly adding olive oil. Rinse chicken; pat dry with paper towels. Arrange rinsed chicken pieces in a single layer in a shallow baking dish; pour marinade over top. Turn chicken to coat both sides. Cover and refrigerate at least 4 hours or overnight, turning once or twice. Remove chicken from refrigerator 30 minutes before barbecuing. Preheat grill; position a wire rack 4 to 6 inches from heat. Remove chicken from marinade, reserving marinade; pat off excess marinade with paper towels. Place marinated chicken on rack. If you are using both dark and light meat, place dark meat on grill 15 minutes before breast or wing pieces; white meat cooks faster than dark meat pieces. Grill 30 to 45 minutes, turning pieces frequently and brushing lightly with reserved marinade. Chicken is done when meat is no longer pink when slashed to bone in thickest portion. Remove cooked chicken to a warm platter. Makes 4 servings.

Variation
Add damp, aromatic, fruitwood chips to fire.

Lemon-Herb Chicken

Fragrant tarragon and rosemary complement chicken with a delicate flavor.

1/3 cup fresh lemon juice
1/4 cup olive oil
1 garlic clove, minced
1 to 2 tablespoon finely chopped fresh
   rosemary or 2 teaspoons dried
   rosemary, crumbled

1 to 2 tablespoons finely chopped fresh
   tarragon or 2 teaspoons dried leaf
   tarragon, crumbled
1 teaspoon salt
1/2 teaspoon freshly ground black pepper
1 (3-1/2-lb.) broiler-fryer chicken, cut up

In a container with a tight-fitting lid or in a small bowl, combine lemon juice, olive oil, garlic, rosemary, tarragon, salt and pepper. Cover container tightly; shake vigorously. Or, in bowl, beat with a whisk until blended. Rinse chicken; pat dry with paper towels. Arrange rinsed chicken in a single layer in a shallow pan; pour marinade over top. Turn chicken to coat both sides. Cover and refrigerate at least 4 hours or overnight, turning once or twice. Remove chicken from refrigerator 30 minutes before barbecuing. Preheat grill; position a wire rack 4 to 6 inches from heat. Remove chicken from marinade, reserving marinade; pat off excess marinade with paper towels. Place marinated chicken on rack. If you are using both dark and light meat, place dark meat on grill 15 minutes before breast or wing pieces; white meat cooks faster than dark meat pieces. Grill 30 to 45 minutes, turning frequently and brushing lightly with reserved marinade. Chicken is done when meat is no longer pink when slashed to bone in thickest portion. Remove cooked chicken to a warm platter. Makes 4 servings.

Charcoal-Roasted Goose with Apple Stuffing

Goose meat is dark, rich and flavorful—an excellent choice for a Sunday or holiday dinner.

4 cups fresh white-bread crumbs
1/4 cup butter or margarine, melted
1/4 cup bacon drippings or
    1/4 cup butter or margarine, melted
4 medium, tart green apples, such as
    Pippin or Granny Smith, peeled,
    finely diced
2 to 3 teaspoons finely chopped
    fresh sage or 1 teaspoon dried sage,
    crumbled

2 to 3 teaspoons finely chopped fresh
    thyme or 1 teaspoon dried leaf thyme,
    crumbled
1 tablespoon finely chopped fresh basil or
    1 teaspoon dried leaf basil, crumbled
1/4 teaspoon ground nutmeg
Salt
Freshly ground black pepper
1 (12- to 14-lb.) goose, thawed if
    frozen, giblets and neck removed

Spread bread crumbs on a baking sheet; let stand at room temperature overnight or until partially dried. Prepare and preheat grill for indirect cooking, page 9. In a large bowl, combine bread crumbs, 1/4 cup butter or margarine, bacon drippings or an additional 1/4 cup butter or margarine, apples, sage, thyme, basil, nutmeg and salt and pepper. Pull out fat from tail area and neck of goose. Rinse goose; pat dry with paper towels. Lightly sprinkle inside of cavity with salt and pepper. Loosely spoon in stuffing until about 3/4 full. Do not pack tightly; stuffing will expand during cooking. Fold wing tips behind shoulder joints and under bird. Truss with heavy string, page 77; sew or skewer cavity closed. Position a wire rack 4 to 6 inches above drip pan. Set goose on rack, breast-side up, over drip pan. Cover grill; open vents slightly. Grill 45 minutes. Turn goose, breast-side down; cover and cook 30 minutes longer. Add more briquets every 45 minutes to maintain a constant temperature. Turn breast-side up; cover and cook about 30 minutes longer or until a meat thermometer inserted in inner-thigh muscle registers 180F to 185F (80C to 85C) or until juices run clear when a knife is inserted between thigh and breast. Remove cooked goose to a carving board. Cover with foil; let stand about 10 minutes before carving. Carve goose; place pieces on a warm platter. Makes 6 to 8 servings.

How to Make a Foil Drip Pan

Using 18-inch-wide heavy foil, tear off a piece of foil twice the length of your grill. Fold the foil in half for a double thickness. Turn up the edges 1-1/2 inches on all sides. Pinch corners together to outside forming triangle shaped corners. Fold corners to sides of pan, making them even with sides. Fold over top of foil edge 1/8 inch all the way around to reinforce the corners.

Smoked Teriyaki Chicken

Soy sauce, sherry, garlic and ginger in the sauce makes this smoked chicken superb.

**1 recipe Teriyaki Marinade, page 102,
   or 1 cup bottled teriyaki marinade
   and sauce**

**1 (5- to 6-lb.) roasting chicken,
   giblets and neck removed**

Prepare Teriyaki Marinade; let stand 1 hour to let flavors blend. Rinse chicken; pat dry with paper towels. Place chicken in a large bowl; pour marinade over top. Turn chicken to coat both sides. Cover and refrigerate 1 to 2 hours, turning 3 or 4 times. Remove chicken from refrigerator 30 minutes before barbecuing. Soak hickory, mesquite or other wood chips in water to cover at least 30 minutes, using 1/4 to 1/2 pound chips for a lightly smoked flavor and 3/4 to 1 pound chips for a smokier flavor. Build a charcoal fire in fire-pan of water-smoker or preheat as manufacturer directs. When coals are low-glowing and covered with a gray ash, spread out in fire-pan. Squeeze water from 1 or 2 handfuls of soaked wood chips; sprinkle on hot coals. Remove chicken from marinade, reserving marinade. Place water-pan over coals; pour marinade and about 2 cups hot water into water-pan. Fold wing tips behind shoulder joints and under birds; truss chicken with heavy string, page 77. Position a wire rack over water-pan; place marinated chicken on rack, breast-side up, above water-pan. Cover smoker; adjust vents as manufacturer directs. Smoke chicken 2 to 3 hours. Add more briquets and soaked wood to fire every 45 minutes to maintain heat and smoke; add more water to water pan, if necessary, to keep it at least 1/2 full. Smoke until a meat thermometer inserted in inner-thigh muscle registers 180F to 185F (80C to 85C) or until juices run clear when a knife is inserted between thigh and breast. Remove smoked chicken to a carving board. Cover with foil; let stand about 10 minutes. Carve chicken; place pieces on a warm platter. Makes 6 servings.

Note: This recipe gives rough guidelines for using a water-smoker. Before starting, read the owner's guide for your smoker, paying particular attention to the amount of water, charcoal and cooking time recommended. If you use an electric or gas smoker without a water-pan, omit liquid used in water-pan; do not soak wood chips. Follow manufacturer's directions for cooking time and adding wood chips.

Grilled Turkeyburgers

A light alternative to hamburgers. Serve with Pesto Tomatoes, page 134, and a fresh fruit salad.

3 tablespoons cold, firm butter or margarine
2 lbs. ground turkey, thaw if frozen
1/4 cup whipping cream
**1/4 cup butter or margarine,
   room temperature**
**2 to 3 teaspoons finely chopped fresh
   tarragon or 3/4 to 1 teaspoon dried leaf
   tarragon, crumbled**

1 teaspoon salt
1/2 teaspoon freshly ground black pepper
6 bacon slices, if desired
6 lemon wedges

Cut 3 tablespoons butter or margarine into 6 pieces; bring to room temperature. Preheat grill; position a wire rack 4 to 6 inches from heat. In a large bowl, combine chicken, cream, 1/4 cup butter or margarine, tarragon, salt and pepper. Shape into 6 patties, each about 3 inches in diameter and 1 inch thick. If desired, wrap a bacon slice around edge of each burger, securing with a small wooden pick. Place burgers on rack. Turning 2 or 3 times, grill 18 to 20 minutes or until well-browned on both sides and burgers are no longer pink when slashed in center. Remove cooked burgers to a warm platter. Top each burger with a pat of room temperature butter; serve each with a lemon wedge. Makes 6 servings.

Smoke-Cooked Turkey with Herb-Butter Baste

This turkey is very juicy, with a light smoky flavor and a rich, golden brown skin.

1 (12- to 15-lb.) turkey, thawed if
   frozen, giblets and neck removed
Salt

Freshly ground black pepper
Herb-Butter Baste, see below
2 cups white wine

Herb-Butter Baste:
1/2 cup butter or margarine
2 tablespoons finely chopped fresh parsley
1 large garlic clove, minced
1-1/2 to 2 teaspoons finely chopped
   fresh thyme or 1/2 teaspoon dried
   leaf thyme, crumbled
1-1/2 to 2 teaspoons finely chopped fresh
   oregano or 1/2 teaspoon dried leaf
   oregano, crumbled

1-1/2 to 2 teaspoons finely chopped fresh
   sage or 1/2 teaspoon dried sage,
   crumbled
1-1/2 to 2 teaspoons finely chopped
   fresh basil or tarragon or
   1/2 teaspoon dried leaf basil or
   tarragon, crumbled

Soak hickory, mesquite or other wood chips in water to cover, at least 30 minutes, using 1/4 to 1/2 pound chips for a lightly smoked flavor and 3/4 to 1 pound chips for a smokier flavor. Build a charcoal fire in fire-pan of water-smoker or preheat as manufacturer directs. When coals are low-glowing and covered with a gray ash, spread out in fire-pan. Rinse turkey; pat dry with paper towels. Season rinsed turkey, inside and out, with salt and pepper. Fold wing tips behind shoulder joints and under bird; truss with heavy string, page 77. Prepare Herb-Butter Baste. Brush turkey with herb butter. Squeeze water from 1 or 2 handfuls of soaked wood chips; sprinkle on hot coals. Place water-pan over coals; pour wine and about 2 cups hot water into water-pan. Position a wire rack over water-pan; place seasoned turkey on rack, breast-side up, above water-pan. Cover smoker; adjust vents as manufacturer directs. Smoke turkey 4 to 6 hours, brushing with herb butter occasionally. Add briquets and soaked wood every 45 minutes to maintain heat and smoke; add more water to water-pan, if necessary, to keep it at least 1/2 full. After 3 hours, insert a meat thermometer in center of inner-thigh muscle. Smoke until thermometer registers 180F to 185F (80C to 85C) or until juices run clear when a knife is inserted between thigh and breast. Remove smoked turkey to a carving board. Cover with foil; let stand about 10 minutes. Carve turkey; place pieces on a warm platter. Makes 12 to 14 servings.

Herb-Butter Baste:
In a small saucepan, melt butter or margarine. Remove from heat; stir in garlic, parsley, thyme, oregano, sage and basil or tarragon.

 TIP *When cooking in a kettle grill, for more moist cooking, add liquid to the drip-pan. Use fruit juice, wine, beer or marinade.*

FISH

Fish is more fragile than meat and poultry, so fish fillets and steaks should be no less than 3/4 to 1 inch thick. Thinner pieces may fall apart on the grill. Turn fish only once, using a wide spatula. A hinged wire basket is handy for cooking whole fish fillets and steaks. Oil the basket to prevent sticking. Foil strips twisted around whole fish, such as in Charcoal-Grilled Fisherman's Catch, also make handles for easy turning.

Take care not to overcook fish. Fish is naturally tender and should be cooked only until the fish firms up and turns opaque throughout. Overcooked fish shrinks, toughens and dries out. You can always grill an undercooked piece of fish longer, but you can't tenderize overcooked food. Check doneness by cutting into the center of the thickest portion. When the flesh becomes slightly opaque, remove fish from the heat. It will continue to cook as it stands. Opacity is also a reliable test of doneness for shellfish.

Fish adapts well to charcoal cookery. You can try your hand at the old standbys—salmon and swordfish steaks, or you can experiment with any firm-textured fish available in your area. Fish with high fat content, such as mackerel, sturgeon, bluefish, mullet and tuna, are especially delicious grilled. The smoky aroma of the charcoal enhances their pronounced flavor and their fat content keeps them moist during cooking. Delicate white fillets, such as flounder and sole, are not suitable for grilling unless done in a skillet, because the flavor of wood and smoke overwhelms them, and they break up easily on the grill.

Although specific types of fish are indicated in the recipes, any firm-textured fish available in your area may be used—salmon, tuna, swordfish and shark are good choices.

Grilled Red Snapper with Butter

True red snapper from the Gulf Coast or Atlantic is firm-textured and delicately sweet.

Almond-Lime Butter, see below
1/2 cup butter or margarine
2 tablespoons chopped fresh dill or
   2 teaspoons dill weed, crumbled

3 lbs. skinless red snapper, rock cod
   or rockfish fillets, about 1 inch thick
Salt
Freshly ground black pepper

Almond-Lime Butter:
1/2 cup whole almonds, toasted
1/2 cup butter or margarine, room temperature

1 lime

Prepare Almond-Lime Butter; refrigerate until served. Preheat grill; position a wire rack 4 to 6 inches from heat. Melt butter or margarine in a small saucepan; remove from heat. Add dill; set aside. Rinse fish; pat dry with paper towels. Lightly season both sides of fish with salt and pepper; cut seasoned fish into 6 pieces. Brush fish pieces with butter-dill mixture; place on rack. Grill 7 to 10 minutes or until fish turns from translucent to opaque throughout, turning once and brushing 2 or 3 times with butter mixture. Remove cooked fish to a warm platter. Cut Almond-Lime Butter into 6 slices; place 1 slice on each serving. Makes 6 servings.

Almond-Lime Butter:
Grate peel from lime; juice lime; set aside. In a food processor fitted with a metal blade, process almonds until coarsely ground. Add butter or margarine, lime peel and lime juice; process until blended. Mound almond-butter mixture on wax paper; shape into a 4-inch-long log. Wrap wax paper around log; refrigerate until firm. Makes about 3/4 cup.

Oriental-Style Tuna

Shoah sing wine, which is found in Oriental markets, is richer and darker than sherry.

1/4 cup soy sauce
2 tablespoons rice vinegar
2 tablespoons shoah sing wine or sherry
8 to 10 thin fresh gingerroot slices
1 large garlic clove, crushed
4 to 5 black peppercorns, coarsely crushed
1/2 teaspoon Oriental sesame oil
1 star anise, if desired

4 (6- to 8-oz.) tuna steaks or other
   firm-textured fish steaks,
   about 1 inch thick
Olive oil or vegetable oil
Cilantro sprigs
1 large red bell pepper,
   cut in thin strips

In a small bowl, combine soy sauce, vinegar, wine or sherry, 6 gingerroot slices, garlic, peppercorns, sesame oil and anise, if desired. Rinse fish; pat dry with paper towels. Arrange rinsed fish in a single layer in a large, shallow baking dish; pour on soy-sauce marinade. Cover and refrigerate 2 to 3 hours, turning once or twice. Remove fish from refrigerator 30 minutes before barbecuing. Preheat grill; position a wire rack 4 to 6 inches from heat. Remove fish from marinade; discard marinade. Pat off excess marinade with paper towels; rub fish lightly with olive oil or vegetable oil. Place oiled fish on rack; grill 7 to 10 minutes or until fish turns from translucent to opaque throughout, turning once. Remove cooked fish to a warm platter; garnish with cilantro, remaining ginger and red-pepper strips. Makes 4 servings.

Shark with Tomato-Pesto Sauce

Shark is a meaty, firm-fleshed fish, and is complemented by a lively pesto sauce.

Tomato-Pesto Sauce, see below
4 (6- to 8-oz.) shark, swordfish or
   tuna steaks, about 1 inch thick

Salt
Freshly ground black pepper
2 tablespoons olive oil

Tomato-Pesto Sauce:

1 large garlic clove
3 tablespoons pine nuts or
   chopped walnuts, toasted
1/3 cup freshly grated Parmesan
   cheese (1 oz.)
1 cup lightly packed fresh basil leaves

1/4 teaspoon freshly ground black pepper
Pinch of red (cayenne) pepper
1/2 teaspoon salt
1/4 cup olive oil
2 medium tomatoes or 4 Italian plum
   tomatoes, peeled, seeded, diced

Prepare Tomato-Pesto Sauce; set aside. Preheat grill; position a wire rack 4 to 6 inches from heat. Rinse fish; pat dry with paper towels. Lightly rub both sides of each steak with olive oil; season with salt and pepper. Place seasoned fish on rack; grill 7 to 10 minutes or until fish turns from translucent to opaque throughout, turning once. Remove cooked fish to a warm platter. Top each with a spoonful of pesto, then a spoonful of chopped tomatoes reserved from pesto. Pour remaining pesto into a small serving bowl; serve separately. Makes 4 servings.

Tomato-Pesto Sauce:

In a blender or food processor fitted with a metal blade, process garlic until finely chopped. Add pine nuts or walnuts, Parmesan cheese, basil, black pepper, red pepper and salt; process until finely chopped. With processor running, add oil to make a smooth paste. Pour pesto into a small bowl; stir in 1/2 of tomatoes. Reserve remaining tomatoes for garnish. Makes about 1/2 cup.

Crispy Cornmeal Catfish

Catfish has a firm flesh and rich flavor—perfect for grilling. Cucumber salad or Old-Fashioned Coleslaw, page 144, makes a tasty accompaniment.

1 recipe Tartar Sauce, page 120
4 to 6 (12-oz.) cleaned skinned catfish
1/2 cup all-purpose flour
1/2 cup yellow cornmeal
1 teaspoon paprika

1 teaspoon salt
1/2 teaspoon freshly ground black pepper
1 egg
1/2 cup milk
4 to 6 lemon wedges

Prepare Tartar Sauce; refrigerate until served. Preheat grill; position a wire rack 4 to 6 inches from heat. Oil 2 square or oblong wire grilling baskets; set aside. On a large plate, combine flour, cornmeal, paprika, salt and pepper. In a shallow bowl, beat egg and milk. Rinse fish; pat dry inside and out with paper towels. Dip catfish, 1 at a time, in egg mixture, turning to coat all sides; roll in cornmeal mixture until evenly coated. Place coated fish in oiled grilling baskets; set on rack or 4 to 6 inches from heat on basket legs. Grill fish 15 to 18 minutes or until well-browned and crisp on both sides, turning once. Carefully open baskets, taking care to keep cornmeal coating intact. Remove cooked fish from baskets; place on a warm platter; arrange lemon wedges around edge of platter. Serve with Tartar Sauce. Makes 4 to 6 servings.

Shark with Tomato-Pesto Sauce; and Tortellini Salad, page 143.

Charcoal-Grilled Fisherman's Catch

Grilling is the ultimate way to cook a fisherman's catch.

Mustard-Herb Butter Sauce, page 109, or
   Garlic-Ginger Butter Sauce, page 109
1 (2-1/2- to 4-lb.) cleaned, scaled,
   whole fish, any type
Salt
Freshly ground black pepper

10 to 15 fresh thyme sprigs or
   1-1/2 to 2 teaspoons dried leaf thyme,
   crumbled
Vegetable oil
Lemon wedges

Preheat grill. Prepare Mustard-Herb Butter or Garlic-Ginger Butter; keep warm on edge of grill. Rinse fish; pat dry with paper towels. Season inside and out with salt and pepper. Place thyme sprigs into fish cavity or sprinkle dried thyme inside fish. Generously rub outside of fish with oil. Cook fish directly on a wire rack or in a hinged wire basket. *To cook on a wire rack,* oil a wire rack; set aside. Tear off 2 (12-inch-long) strips of heavy foil. Fold each strip in half lengthwise, 4 times. Grease one side of strips. Place 1 strip under each end of fish, greased-side against fish. Fold strips around fish, twisting at belly to make handles for turning. Place fish on greased rack; position rack 4 to 6 inches from heat. *To cook fish in a hinged wire basket,* generously oil basket. Place fish in oiled grilling basket; set 4 to 6 inches from heat on a wire rack or on basket legs. Cover grill; open vents slightly. Grill 5 to 10 minutes; remove cover and turn fish. Cover and cook 5 to 10 minutes longer or until fish turns from transparent to opaque in thickest portion. Remove cooked fish to a warm platter; serve with Mustard-Herb Butter or Garlic-Ginger Butter. Makes 4 to 6 servings.

Grilled Sea Bass

Mint complements the flavor of this firm-textured fish.

1/4 cup butter or margarine
2 large garlic cloves, minced
3 tablespoons finely chopped fresh mint
2 tablespoons fresh lemon juice
2 tablespoons finely chopped green onion
   with tops

4 (6- to 8-oz.) sea bass steaks,
   about 1 inch thick
Salt
Freshly ground black pepper

Preheat grill; position a wire rack 4 to 6 inches from heat. In a small saucepan, melt butter or margarine. Remove from heat; stir in garlic, mint, lemon juice and green onion. Set aside. Rinse fish; pat dry with paper towels. Lightly season both sides of fish with salt and pepper. Brush fish lightly with butter mixture; place buttered fish on rack. Grill 5 minutes; turn and brush with butter mixture. Grill 2 to 5 minutes longer or until fish turns from translucent to opaque throughout. Remove cooked fish to a warm platter. Makes 4 servings.

Variation
If sea bass is unavailable, substitute other firm-textured steaks or fillets, such as halibut, cod, shark or swordfish, about 1 inch thick.

Sea Bass with Cilantro Sauce

A mild, firm-textured fish, served with a thick, pungent sauce.

Cilantro Sauce, see below
1-1/2 to 2 lbs. skinless sea bass,
  3/4 to 1 inch thick

2 to 3 tablespoons olive oil
Salt
Freshly ground black pepper

Cilantro Sauce:
1 cup loosely packed cilantro sprigs
  (coriander or Chinese parsley)
3/4 cup coarsely chopped green onions
  with tops
2 tablespoons fresh lemon juice
2 jalapeño peppers, seeded,
  coarsely chopped

1/4 teaspoon ground cinnamon
1/4 teaspoon ground cloves
1/4 teaspoon ground cumin
1/4 teaspoon ground turmeric
1/4 cup olive oil

Prepare Cilantro Sauce; refrigerate until served. Preheat grill; position a wire rack 4 to 6 inches from heat. Rinse fish; pat dry with paper towels. Cut fish into 4 equal pieces. Rub both sides lightly with olive oil; season with salt and pepper. Place seasoned fish pieces on rack. Grill 7 to 10 minutes or until fillets turn from translucent to opaque throughout, turning once. Remove cooked fish to a warm platter; place a small spoonful of sauce on top of each. Pour remaining sauce into a small serving dish; serve separately. Makes 4 servings.

Cilantro Sauce:

In a food processor fitted with a metal blade, combine cilantro, green onions, lemon juice, jalapeño peppers, cinnamon, cloves, cumin and turmeric. Process with on/off motions until ingredients are finely chopped, stopping 2 or 3 times to scrape down bowl. With processor running, slowly add olive oil; process to make a thick paste. Makes about 3/4 cup.

Bacon-Wrapped Trout

Pungent horseradish complements the flavor of the rosemary-scented fish and smoky bacon.

Horseradish Cream, see below
4 (8-oz.) cleaned whole trout
Salt
Freshly ground black pepper

1/3 cup chopped walnuts, toasted
4 fresh rosemary sprigs or 1 to 1-1/2
    teaspoons dried rosemary, crumbled
12 bacon slices (about 3/4 lb.)

Horseradish Cream:
1/2 cup whipping cream
3/4 to 1 teaspoons sugar
2 to 3 tablespoons grated fresh horseradish

1/2 to 1 tablespoon white-wine vinegar
Salt
Freshly ground white pepper

Prepare Horseradish Cream; set aside. Preheat grill; position a wire rack 4 to 6 inches from heat. Rinse fish; pat dry with paper towels. Lightly season cavity of each fish with salt and pepper. Spread a generous tablespoon of walnuts inside each seasoned fish; insert a rosemary sprig or about 1/4 teaspoon of dried rosemary in each. Wrap 3 bacon slices around each fish, securing with a small wooden pick. Place bacon-wrapped fish on rack. Grill 15 to 20 minutes, turning 2 or 3 times, until ends of bacon are crisp and fish turns from translucent to opaque in thickest portion. If you like bacon more crisp, remove from fish. Place cooked fish on edge of grill to keep warm. Place bacon on center of grill to cook a few minutes longer. Remove cooked fish to a warm platter; serve with grilled bacon and Horseradish Cream. Makes 4 servings.

Horseradish Cream:
In a medium bowl, whip cream and sugar until soft peaks form. Fold horseradish and vinegar into whipped-cream mixture. Season to taste with salt and white pepper. Spoon sauce into a small serving bowl; cover and refrigerate at least 1 hour or up to 4 hours. Makes about 3/4 cup.

Variation
To substitute prepared horseradish for fresh horseradish, omit sugar and vinegar from recipe. Whip cream as directed above; stir in 1 to 2 tablespoons prepared horseradish. For a stronger flavor, use more horseradish.

Grilled Trout

You'll love this delicate, sweet-flavored trout seasoned with butter, salt and pepper.

6 (8-oz.) cleaned whole trout
Salt
Freshly ground black pepper

1/2 cup butter or margarine, melted
Lemon wedges
Parsley sprigs

Preheat grill; position a wire rack 4 to 6 inches from heat. Rinse fish; pat dry with paper towels. Lightly season cavity of each fish with salt and pepper. Place seasoned fish on rack. Grill 10 to 12 minutes or until skin is lightly browned and blistered in spots and flesh turns from transparent to opaque throughout, turning 2 or 3 times and brushing occasionally with butter or margarine. Remove cooked fish to a warm platter; garnish with lemon wedges and parsley sprigs. Makes 6 servings.

Corn-Husked Trout

Wrapping the trout in corn husks keeps it moist and delicious.

6 large ears of corn with husks
6 (8-oz.) cleaned whole trout
6 tablespoons butter or margarine,
   room temperature
Salt
Freshly ground black pepper

6 small fresh tarragon sprigs or
   1 to 1-1/2 teaspoons dried leaf
   tarragon, crumbled
1/2 cup butter or margarine, melted
Lemon wedges
Watercress sprigs

Preheat grill; position a wire rack 4 to 6 inches from heat. Cut stems off corn. Being careful not to tear husks, remove husks from corn; remove and discard silk and set corn and husks aside. Rinse fish; pat dry with paper towels. Spread cavity of each fish with 1 tablespoon room temperature butter or margarine; sprinkle with salt and pepper. Insert a tarragon sprig or about 1/4 teaspoon dried tarragon into each fish cavity. Lay 3 large corn husks on a flat surface, overlapping slightly. Place a seasoned fish on top; cover with 3 more husks. Because husks curl, have someone help you with the next step. Tie a 12-inch piece of heavy string around center of husk-wrapped fish. Tie again around tail and close to head. Brush husked corn with melted butter; season with salt and pepper. Place seasoned corn around edge of wire rack. Place wrapped fish in a single layer in center of rack. Grill 12 to 15 minutes. Brush corn several times with butter; turn both fish and corn 2 or 3 times. Watch carefully because corn burns easily. Remove cooked fish and corn to a warm platter; garnish with lemon wedges and watercress. Let each guest unwrap their own fish. Makes 6 servings.

Halibut with Green-Chile Sauce

A lovely contrast between a mild white fish and a spicy emerald chili sauce.

Green-Chile Sauce, see below
4 (6- to 8-oz.) halibut steaks,
   about 1 inch thick

2 to 3 tablespoons olive oil
Salt
Freshly ground black pepper

Green-Chile Sauce:

1 (4-oz.) can diced chilies
1 fresh Anaheim chili pepper, if desired,
   seeded, coarsely chopped
1/4 cup fresh cilantro sprigs
   (coriander or Chinese parsley)

2 small garlic cloves
1 tablespoon chopped onion
2 thin fresh gingerroot slices
1/4 cup white-wine vinegar
1/4 teaspoon salt

Prepare Green-Chile Sauce; refrigerate until served. Preheat grill; position a wire rack 4 to 6 inches from heat. Rinse fish; pat dry with paper towels. Rub both sides lightly with olive oil; season with salt and pepper. Place seasoned fish on rack; grill 5 minutes. Turn and continue grilling 2 to 5 minutes longer or until fish turns from translucent to opaque. Remove cooked fish to a warm platter; place a small spoonful of sauce on top of each. Spoon remaining sauce into a small serving dish; serve separately. Makes 4 servings.

Green-Chile Sauce:
In a food processor fitted with a metal blade, combine all ingredients. Process with on/off motions until ingredients are smooth, stopping 2 or 3 times to scrape down bowl. Makes about 1/2 cup.

Smoked Salmon

This mild, smoky flavored fish smokes 90 minutes but remains moist.

1 tablespoon soy sauce
2 tablespoons olive oil
1 (3- to 5-lb.) center-cut salmon piece,
  bone-in, skin intact
1 to 2 teaspoons dill weed or several
  fresh dill or fennel sprigs

1/2 teaspoon freshly ground black pepper
3 cups dry white wine, if desired
Cucumber Sauce, page 114, if desired
Blender Mayonnaise, page 121, if desired

In a small bowl, combine soy sauce and olive oil; set aside. Rinse fish; pat dry with paper towels. Place fish on a large platter or baking sheet; rub outside of fish with soy-sauce mixture. Sprinkle cavity of fish with dried dill or insert several fresh dill or fennel sprigs in cavity; then sprinkle with pepper. Soak apple, alder or other mild wood chips in water to cover, at least 30 minutes, using 1/4 to 1/2 pound chips for a lightly smoked flavor and 3/4 to 1 pound chips for a smokier flavor. Build a charcoal fire in fire-pan of water-smoker or preheat as manufacturer directs. When coals are low-glowing and covered with a gray ash, spread out in fire pan. Squeeze water from 1 or 2 handfuls of soaked wood chips; sprinkle on hot coals. Set water-pan on rack over coals. Pour wine in water-pan, if desired; add 3 cups water. Or, fill water-pan with 6 cups water. Position a wire rack over water-pan; place seasoned fish on rack. Cover smoker; adjust vents as manufacturer directs. Smoke fish 1-1/2 hours. Add briquets and soaked wood every 45 minutes to maintain heat and smoke; add more water to water-pan if necessary to keep it at least 1/2 full. After smoking 1 hour, remove water-pan; cover and cook 30 minutes longer or until a meat thermometer inserted in thickest part of flesh without touching bone reaches 140F (60C). Meanwhile, prepare Cucumber Sauce; set aside. Remove cooked fish to a warm platter. Cover with foil; let stand about 10 minutes. Serve with Cucumber Sauce or Blender Mayonnaise. Makes 6 to 10 servings.

Spiced Rockfish with Browned Butter

Browned butter sauce and golden spices give this grilled fish a rich, auburn color.

1/2 cup unsalted butter
1-1/2 to 2 lbs. skinless rockfish,
  rock cod or red snapper fillets,
  3/4 to 1 inch thick
1 tablespoon ground coriander
1 teaspoon ground cumin

1 teaspoon ground turmeric
1/2 teaspoon ground cinnamon
1/2 teaspoon ground cloves
1 teaspoon freshly ground black pepper
1/8 teaspoon red (cayenne) pepper
1/4 cup vegetable oil

Preheat grill; position a wire rack 4 to 6 inches from heat. In a small saucepan, melt butter on grill; swirl pan gently until butter turns a golden walnut brown. Set browned butter aside on edge of grill. Rinse fish; pat dry with paper towels. Cut fish into 4 equal pieces. In a small bowl, combine coriander, cumin, turmeric, cinnamon, cloves, black pepper and red pepper. Rub both sides of fish pieces lightly with oil; season with spice mixture. Place seasoned fish on rack; grill 7 to 10 minutes or until fish turns from translucent to opaque, turning once. Remove cooked fish to a warm platter; top with browned butter. Makes 4 servings.

How to Make Smoked Salmon

1/Insert several fresh dill sprigs in salmon cavity; set aside while soaking aromatic wood chips for barbecue.

2/After 90 minutes of smoking, the still moist, but firm-textured salmon is ready to eat. Serve warm or at room temperature accompanied with lemon slices and crunchy Cucumber Sauce.

Smoked Trout

Smoked trout are perfect picnic food—even better a day or two after they're smoked. Although fish is cooked longer than usual, it does not dry out, but develops a subtle smoky flavor.

4 (8-oz.) cleaned whole trout
2 tablespoons vegetable oil

Herb Rub for Fish, page 110
12 thin lemon slices

Rinse trout; pat dry with paper towels. Rub trout lightly inside and out with oil. Rub 1/4 of dry rub over outside and in cavity of fish. Cover and refrigerate 30 to 60 minutes. Meanwhile, soak apple, alder or other mild wood chips or grapevine cuttings in water to cover, at least 30 minutes, using 1/4 to 1/2 pound chips for a lightly smoked flavor and 3/4 to 1 pound chips for a smokier flavor. Build a charcoal fire in fire-pan of water-smoker or preheat as manufacturer directs. Squeeze water from 1 or 2 handfuls of wood chips or grapevine cuttings; sprinkle over hot coals. No water-pan is used in this recipe because smoked fish will be too moist. Because trout is delicate, fire in smoker should be quite low or fish will cook before it absorbs much of smoky flavor. Place seasoned trout on wire rack. Cover smoker; smoke fish 1 hour and 15 minutes. About every 20 minutes, add a few more pieces of soaked wood to fire. Add briquets about every 45 minutes to maintain heat. Remove cooked fish to a warm platter. Serve hot, or cool slightly; cover and refrigerate until served, up to 48 hours. Makes 4 servings.

Monkfish with Salsa

The strong flavor and firm texture of monkfish stands up well to a fresh salsa.

3 lbs. skinless monkfish fillets or
    other angler fillets, 1 inch thick
1/3 cup olive oil
2 tablespoons fresh lemon juice or
    lime juice
2 garlic cloves, minced
2 teaspoons chopped fresh oregano or
    1/2 teaspoon dried leaf oregano,
    crumbled

1 teaspoon salt
1/2 teaspoon freshly ground black pepper
1 recipe Fresh Salsa from Fresh Salsa &
    Toasted Tortillas, page 123

Rinse fish; pat dry with paper towels. Cut fish into 6 equal pieces. Arrange fish pieces in a single layer in a large, shallow baking dish. In a small bowl, whisk together olive oil, lemon juice or lime juice, garlic, oregano, salt and pepper. Pour marinade over fish. Cover and refrigerate 1 to 2 hours, turning once. Prepare Fresh Salsa; refrigerate until served. Remove fish from refrigerator 30 minutes before barbecuing. Preheat grill; position a wire rack 4 to 6 inches from heat. Remove fish from marinade, reserving marinade; pat off excess marinade with paper towels. Place marinated fish on rack; grill 5 to 7 minutes, turning once and brushing with reserved marinade. Cover grill; open vents slightly. Cook 5 to 10 minutes longer or until fish turns from translucent to opaque throughout. Remove cooked fish to a warm platter; serve with Fresh Salsa. Makes 6 to 8 servings.

Fennel-Marinated Salmon

This delightful flavor combination will have you asking for more. Serve with grilled vegetables or sautéed cucumbers and boiled new potatoes.

3 tablespoons fennel seeds
1/2 cup olive oil
1 teaspoon freshly ground black pepper
2 tablespoons anise-flavored liqueur,
    such as Pernod, or brandy

4 (6- to 8-oz.) salmon steaks or
    fillets, about 1 inch thick

Place fennel seeds in a small cast-iron skillet. Toast over medium-high heat about 3 minutes, stirring until seeds are lightly browned. Crush warm seeds slightly with a mortar and pestle, or pour seeds onto a saucer and crush with the back of a spoon. In a small bowl, combine crushed fennel seeds, olive oil and pepper; whisk in liqueur or brandy. Rinse fish; pat dry with paper towels. Arrange rinsed fish in a baking pan large enough to hold fish in a single layer. Pour oil mixture over fish; turn to coat all sides. Cover and refrigerate 3 to 4 hours, turning once or twice. Preheat grill; position a wire rack 4 to 6 inches from heat. Remove fish from marinade, reserving marinade; pat off excess marinade with paper towels. Place marinated fish on rack; grill 7 to 10 minutes or until fish turns from translucent to opaque, turning once and brushing occasionally with reserved marinade. Remove cooked fish to a warm platter. Makes 4 servings.

Variation
Add damp alder chips to hot coals, if desired, page 8.

Frozen Fish Fillets with Butter Sauce

Sauté these fillets while they are still frozen. Some packages of frozen fish have wrapped individual fillets; others have pieces frozen together in mass. If you purchase a package with a solid mass of fillets, thaw slightly, then break apart fillets.

2 tablespoons butter or margarine	Salt
2 tablespoons vegetable oil	Freshly ground black pepper
1 (12-oz.) pkg. frozen sole, flounder or	3 to 4 tablespoons fresh lemon juice
other white fish fillets, thawed slightly,	4 teaspoons capers
if necessary	Fresh parsley sprigs

Preheat grill; position a wire rack 4 to 6 inches from heat. In a large cast-iron skillet, on rack, heat butter or margarine and oil until bubbly. Arrange frozen fillets in a single layer in skillet. Sauté 2 to 3 minutes on each side (if slightly thawed, sauté 1-2 minutes), or until lightly browned around edges and fish turns from translucent to opaque. Sprinkle with salt, pepper, lemon juice and capers. Remove cooked fish to a warm platter or individual plates. Spoon sauce and capers over top. Garnish with parsley sprigs. Serve immediately. Makes 4 servings.

Japanese Grilled Halibut

Rubbing food lightly with salt is typical of Japanese grilling, giving a very moist fish. The dipping sauce can be prepared ahead; it becomes hotter in taste the further in advance it's made.

Dipping Sauce, see below	Salt
4 (6- to 8-oz.) halibut steaks,	2 red bell peppers
about 1 inch thick	2 yellow, red or green bell peppers

Dipping Sauce:
1/2 cup rice vinegar
3 or 4 dry, hot Thai red peppers or
   2 to 3 teaspoons crushed red-pepper
   flakes

Prepare Dipping Sauce. Rinse fish; pat dry with paper towels. Sprinkle fish lightly with salt; rub in salt. Place salted fish in a shallow baking dish; cover and refrigerate 1 hour. Meanwhile, preheat oven broiler. Line a large, shallow baking pan or baking sheet with foil to make clean-up easier. Place bell peppers in a single layer in pan; place 2 to 4 inches under broiler. Broil until peppers are blistered on all sides, turning often with long-handled tongs. When peppers are charred and puffed all over, remove from broiler. Let stand at room temperature until cool enough to handle; strip off peel with your fingers or tip of a knife. Do not rinse peeled peppers because flavor will be lost. Cut peeled peppers into 1/4-inch-wide strips; set aside. Preheat grill; position a wire rack 4 to 6 inches from heat. Remove salted fish from refrigerator 15 to 20 minutes before grilling. Place salted fish on rack; grill 7 to 10 minutes, turning once, until fish turns from translucent to opaque. Remove cooked fish to a warm platter; garnish with roasted pepper strips. Serve with Dipping Sauce. Makes 4 servings.

Dipping Sauce:
In a container with a tight-fitting lid, combine vinegar and red peppers or crushed red-pepper flakes; cover tightly. Cover and refrigerate 3 to 4 hours. Makes about 1/2 cup.

Skewered Scallops & Mushrooms

Grill scallops quickly, then serve them immediately.

2 lbs. sea scallops
1/2 cup olive oil
1/4 cup fresh lemon juice
1/4 cup chopped fresh cilantro
   (coriander or Chinese parsley)
1 teaspoon salt

1/2 teaspoon freshly ground black pepper
1 lb. medium mushrooms, stems removed
Watercress sprigs
Lemon wedges

Rinse scallops; pat dry with paper towels. In a medium bowl, whisk together olive oil, lemon juice, cilantro, salt and pepper. Add rinsed scallops and mushrooms; toss to coat. Cover and refrigerate 30 minutes. Preheat grill; position a wire rack 4 to 6 inches from heat. Remove scallops and mushrooms from marinade, reserving marinade. Thread marinated scallops and mushrooms alternately on 8 to 12 long thin metal skewers. Place skewers on rack; grill 4 to 8 minutes or until scallops turn from translucent to opaque, turning 3 or 4 times and brushing with reserved marinade. Remove cooked skewered scallops and mushrooms to a large platter. Garnish platter with watercress and lemon wedges. Makes 4 to 6 servings.

Grilled Lobster Tails

When it comes to lobster, the simplest method of grilling is best. Do not overcook lobster or it will toughen.

4 (8-oz.) frozen uncooked lobster
   tails, thawed

1 cup butter, melted
Lemon wedges

Preheat grill; position a wire rack 4 to 6 inches from heat. Oil a square or oblong wire grilling basket; set aside. To prepare lobster, cut along edges of soft undershell with kitchen shears. Clip off fins along outer edges. Peel back and discard soft undershell. Bend tail backward, cracking several joints in hard overshell to prevent curling. Pour about 1/4 cup butter into a small dish to use while grilling; reserve remaining butter to serve later. Brush lobster with butter. Place tails, shell-side down, on greased wire rack; position rack 4 to 6 inches from heat. Cover grill; open vents slightly. Grill 5 minutes; brush with butter and turn lobster. Cover and grill 3 to 5 minutes longer or until flesh is opaque in thickest portion. Remove cooked lobster to a warm platter; garnish with lemon wedges. Serve with remaining butter. Makes 4 servings.

How to Make Grilled Squid

1/Cut off tentacles above eyes. Squeeze out hard round beak from base of tentacles; discard beak and set tentacles aside. Either leave on the thin, transparent, speckled membrane or with your fingers, pull off and discard; rinse and drain mantle.

2/Finely chop tentacles and prepare filling. Spoon 1-1/2 to 2 tablespoons into each mantle cavity; close opening with a wooden skewer.

Grilled Squid

Squid cooks in a flash but toughens when overcooked, so watch it carefully.

12 medium squid, thawed, if frozen
1/2 cup butter or margarine,
  room temperature
1/4 cup finely chopped fresh parsley
1/4 cup finely chopped shallots or
  white parts of green onions

Salt
1/4 teaspoon or more red (cayenne)
  pepper
Olive oil

Preheat grill; position a wire rack 4 to 6 inches from heat. To clean squid, hold body in one hand and base of tentacles just above eyes in other hand. Pull gently to separate body and tentacles. Pull out transparent sword-shaped quill from body. Pull out and discard viscera and ink sac, then rinse body cavity. Cut off tentacles just above the eyes; reserve tentacles. Squeeze small, hard round beak from base of tentacles; discard beak. Leave transparent purple-speckled membrane covering body, or carefully pull off and discard. Pat bodies and tentacles dry with paper towels. Finely chop tentacles; place in a medium bowl. Stir in butter or margarine, parsley, shallots or green onions, salt and 1/4 teaspoon red pepper. Spoon 1-1/2 to 2 teaspoons butter mixture inside each squid body; close opening with a small wooden pick. Rub bodies lightly with olive oil. Place stuffed squid on rack; grill 30 to 45 seconds on each side or until bodies turn from transparent to opaque throughout. Remove cooked squid to a warm platter. Makes 4 servings.

Spicy Skewered Shrimp

Shrimp are entirely edible, shells and all, although the timid may want to shell them.

2/3 cup olive oil or 1/3 cup olive oil
and 1/3 cup vegetable oil
1 tablespoon ground turmeric
1/4 teaspoon freshly ground black
pepper
3 garlic cloves, minced
1 tablespoon finely chopped fresh basil or
1 teaspoon dried leaf basil, crumbled

1 tablespoon finely chopped fresh mint or
1 teaspoon dried leaf mint, crumbled
1-1/2 teaspoons red (cayenne) pepper
1 tablespoons red-wine vinegar
2 lbs. large shrimp (20 to 32), unshelled

In a large bowl, whisk together olive oil or combination of oils, turmeric, black pepper, garlic, basil, mint, red pepper and vinegar. Rinse shrimp; pat dry with paper towels. Toss shrimp in marinade to coat. Cover and refrigerate 6 to 8 hours or overnight, tossing occasionally. Remove shrimp from refrigerator 30 minutes before barbecuing. Preheat grill; position a wire rack 4 to 6 inches from heat. Remove shrimp from marinade, reserving marinade. Thread marinated shrimp on 12 long metal skewers; place on rack. Grill shrimp 3 to 5 minutes until shrimp turn pink, turning 3 or 4 times and basting with reserved marinade. Remove cooked shrimp to a warm platter; serve immediately while still hot. Shells become more crisp as they cool. Makes about 6 to 8 servings.

Shrimp Sauté

After sautéing shrimp, grill red Italian lettuce or red-cabbage leaves for a garnish. Radicchio is somewhat like lettuce, but is sturdier and has a slightly bitter taste.

1 lb. large or jumbo shrimp, shelled,
deveined (16 to 25)
Salt
Freshly ground black pepper
2 tablespoons butter or margarine
2 tablespoons vegetable oil
2 tablespoons minced shallots

1/2 teaspoon minced fresh green
Anaheim chili pepper
3 to 4 tablespoons fresh lemon juice
1 head Italian radicchio or red cabbage,
separated into leaves
Several cilantro sprigs (coriander or
Chinese parsley)

Preheat grill; position a wire rack 4 to 6 inches from heat. Butterfly jumbo shrimp; sprinkle with salt and pepper. In a large cast-iron skillet, on rack, heat butter or margarine and oil until bubbly. Add shrimp; sauté 2 to 3 minutes on each side or until browned and shrimp turn pink. Move shrimp to one side of skillet. Add shallots; sauté until soft, moving skillet off direct heat if too hot. Stir in chili pepper and lemon juice; remove skillet from grill. Place individual radicchio or cabbage leaves on grill; cook 10 to 15 seconds on each side or until hot and leaves begin to change color. Remove hot leaves to a warm platter. Top leaves with grilled shrimp. Spoon sauce over top. Garnish with Chinese parsley or cilantro sprigs. Serve immediately. Makes 2 to 4 servings.

Spicy Skewered Shrimp, and skewered marinated mushrooms and artichokes.

Clams Steamed in Wine & Herbs

A light and flavorful first course.

4 lbs. littleneck or steamer clams
   (about 4 qts. or 80 clams)
1/4 cup butter or margarine
1 cup finely chopped onion
1/4 cup chopped green onions

2 or 3 large garlic cloves, minced
1 bay leaf
1/4 cup finely chopped fresh parsley
2 cups dry white wine
French or Italian bread

Scrub clams under cold running water. Discard clams that remain open. Place scrubbed clams in a large basin of cold water; let soak at least 30 minutes. Preheat grill, keeping coals close together to make a hot concentrated fire. Position a wire rack 4 to 6 inches from heat. Drain clams; set aside. Place a 6- to 8-quart kettle or Dutch oven on rack. Add butter or margarine; when melted, add onion, green onions and garlic. Sauté 5 to 10 minutes or until soft. Stir in bay leaf, parsley and drained clams; pour in wine. Cover grill. If cover will not fit over pot, cover with a tent of foil, page 66. Cook clams 5 to 7 minutes; if any shells remain unopened, cook 2 to 3 minutes longer. Discard any unopened shells and bay leaf. Ladle opened clams and their cooking liquid into a large serving bowl or individual soup bowls. Serve immediately with sliced crusty French bread or Italian bread. Makes 4 to 6 servings.

Nancy's Clambake

A streamlined version of a New England feast you can prepare in a large covered smoker.

1-1/2 lbs. (about 30) littleneck or
   steamer clams
1-1/2 lbs. (about 30) mussels,
   debearded
3 (2-1/2- to 3-lb.) broiler-fryer
   chickens, quartered
6 baking potatoes, scrubbed

6 large ears of fresh corn, shucked
Sea water or tap water
2 cups white wine, if desired
Several handfuls of washed seaweed or
   bunches of fresh thyme, tarragon or
   rosemary, if desired
Butter, melted
Crusty bread

Scrub clams and mussels under cold running water. Discard clams that remain open. Combine scrubbed clams and mussels in a large basin of cold water; soak for 30 to 60 minutes. Meanwhile, wrap chicken in cheesecloth; wrap each potato and ear of corn in individual pieces of foil. Drain clams and mussels; set aside. Prepare a large charcoal fire in smoker. When coals are low-glowing and covered with a gray ash, spread out in fire-pan. Place water-pan over coals; fill with water. Position a wire rack over water-pan; cover smoker until water is boiling. Remove cover; drop several handfuls of seaweed or bunches of fresh herbs into boiling water. Place foil-wrapped potatoes and wrapped chicken on rack above water-pan. Cover and cook 30 minutes; place wrapped corn on top of potatoes and chickens. Cover and cook 15 minutes longer; distribute drained clams and mussels over top. Cover and cook 5 to 10 minutes longer or until clams and mussels have opened. If any shells remain unopened, cook 2 to 3 minutes longer. Discard any unopened shells. Place cooked clams and mussels in a large bowl; mound wrapped chicken, potatoes and corn on large platters. Let guests unwrap their own vegetables and chicken. Serve melted butter for dipping and lots of crusty bread for sopping up juices. Makes 6 to 12 servings.

How to Make Shrimp Kabobs

1/Peel raw shrimp leaving tails intact. To remove sand vein, make a shallow cut from tail to head down back of shrimp; rinse out sand vein under cold running water.

2/Insert a wooden skewer, lengthwise, into body of 2 shrimp; skewer remaining shrimp, 2 per skewer. Shrimp are done when they turn a coral pink. Serve hot with dipping sauces.

Shrimp Kabobs with Dipping Sauces

Allow 4 to 6 shrimp per person for an appetizer.

**Cocktail Dipping Sauce and
  Mustard-Dill Dipping Sauce, page 112**

**1-1/2 lbs. medium shrimp (25 to 40)
Butter or margarine, melted**

Prepare Cocktail Dipping Sauce and Mustard-Dill Dipping Sauce; set aside. Place about 36 (4-inch) bamboo skewers in a 9'' x 5'' loaf pan. Cover with water; let soak at least 30 minutes. Preheat grill; position a wire grill 4 to 6 inches from heat. Shell shrimp leaving tails attached; devein shrimp by inserting a wooden skewer or pick beneath vein and carefully pulling it out. Push a soaked skewer lengthwise into body of each shrimp, starting beneath tail. Brush skewered shrimp with butter or margarine. Place on rack; grill 4 to 8 minutes until shrimp turn pink, turning skewers once or twice. Remove cooked shrimp to a warm platter; serve shrimp with dipping sauces. Makes 6 to 8 appetizer servings.

SAUCES, MARINADES & BUTTERS

Many popular finger-lickin' barbecue sauces are tomato-based—using ketchup, tomato sauce or chili sauce. They not only make delicious basting sauces or marinades, but are excellent table sauces as well.

Marinades heighten flavor and tenderize meat. They are usually made with oil and some acid or alcohol such as wine, beer, fruit juice or vinegar. Oil lubricates the meat's surface and keeps it from sticking to the wire rack. An efficient way to marinate meat is to place it in a large, heavy plastic food-storage bag and pour in the marinade. Close the bag airtight and press the marinade into the meat. Place the bag in a large bowl to catch any leaks or drips.

Wine, vinegar or lemon marinades are excellent tenderizers because their acidity breaks down the connective tissue of meat. For best results, marinate meat 2 to 3 hours or overnight. Meat marinated at room temperature will take on the flavor of the marinade more quickly than if marinated in the refrigerator, but should never be left at room temperature longer than 1 hour.

To prevent burning, begin brushing tomato- or sugar-based sauces or marinades on meat 10 to 15 minutes before it is removed from the grill, unless you cook meat slowly in a covered kettle. Then the sauce can be brushed on during the last hour.

Dry rubs, a form of marinade, are a mixture of sugar, salt and seasonings that are rubbed into the meat before cooking. The rub seals the surface of the meat as it cooks. Salt in the dry rub combines with meat juices to create a brine that penetrates and flavors the meat. Even when only marinated 15 to 30 minutes in a salty dry rub, beef flavor improves greatly. Rinse off the dry rub before cooking the meat, if desired.

Butters—hot butter sauces, butter purees and compound butters—offer endless combinations of flavors. Compound butters are simply softened butters flavored with herbs and seasonings. Spoon a dollop of the softened mixture onto hot grilled meat or vegetables, or shape the butter into logs, chill, and cut into pats. Hot butter sauces are quick to make and are a good standby for plain grilled foods. Butter purees are versatile—use them as as a basting sauce or let them firm-up at room temperature and spoon them like compound butters.

Spicy Plum Barbecue Sauce

Can this spicy sauce in fancy jars. It makes a great gift for barbecue fans.

2 tablespoons vegetable oil
1 medium onion, chopped
4 large garlic cloves, minced
3 lbs. red plums, pitted, coarsely chopped
3/4 cup sugar

1/4 cup soy sauce
1/4 cup fresh lemon juice
2 teaspoons or more curry powder
3/4 teaspoon ground cinnamon
1/4 teaspoon red (cayenne) pepper

Heat oil in a large heavy saucepan. Add onion and garlic; sauté until onion is soft. Stir in remaining ingredients. Bring to a simmer. Simmer 45 to 60 minutes or until mixture is thick and reduced to about 4 cups, stirring frequently the last 10 minutes of cooking to prevent sticking and scorching. Use immediately, can in 1/2-pint jars or cool slightly and pour into a container with a tight-fitting lid. Cover tightly; refrigerate up to 3 weeks. **To can,** ladle hot sauce into clean, hot 1/2-pint canning jars, leaving 1/2 inch headspace. Wipe rims of jars with a clean damp cloth. Close jars with metal lids and ring bands. Place in a pot or kettle of boiling water, being sure that water covers lids. Cover pot; bring water to a full boil. Begin counting processing time. At altitudes under 1000 feet, boil 20 minutes. Add 1 minute at 1000 feet; add 1 minute for each additional 1000 feet. Makes 4 cups or 4 (1/2-pint) jars.

All-American Barbecue Sauce

A tangy red sauce, not too tart and not too sweet—serve with meat and poultry.

2 tablespoons butter or margarine
1 onion, finely chopped
1 large garlic clove, minced
1-1/4 cups ketchup
1/3 cup lightly packed brown sugar

1/4 cup Worcestershire sauce
2 teaspoons chili powder
Dash of red-pepper sauce
1/3 cup cider vinegar

Melt butter or margarine in a medium saucepan. Add onion and garlic; sauté until onion is soft. Stir in remaining ingredients. Bring sauce to a simmer; simmer 15 minutes or until slightly thickened. Remove from heat; cover and let stand at least 1 hour to let flavors blend. Use immediately or pour into a container with a tight-fitting lid. Cool then cover tightly; refrigerate up to 7 days. Use to brush on meats as they grill or serve with grilled meats. Makes about 2-1/4 cups.

TIP *Mop sops and other barbecue sauces are applied with a long-handled basting brush or small cotton "mop," such as those used for washing dishes. Many barbecue cooks have a "mop" reserved for this purpose only.*

Teriyaki Marinade

An Oriental soy-and-ginger marinade for all kinds of poultry, beef, pork and dense fish.

1/2 cup soy sauce
1/3 cup dry sherry
1/4 cup vegetable oil
1/4 cup sugar

2 large garlic cloves, minced
2 teaspoons grated fresh gingerroot or
  1 teaspoon ground ginger

In a small bowl, whisk all ingredients together. Cover and let stand at least 1 hour to let flavors blend. If not using immediately, pour into a container with a tight-fitting lid. Cover tightly; refrigerate up to 7 days. Makes about 1 cup or enough marinade for 3 pounds meat, fish or poultry.

Lemon-Basil Marinade

A tangy marinade for chicken or veal.

1 large lemon
1/2 cup olive oil
1/2 cup finely chopped fresh basil or
  3 tablespoons dried leaf basil, crumbled

1 teaspoon salt
1/2 teaspoon freshly ground black pepper

Grate peel from lemon; squeeze juice from lemon. In a medium bowl, whisk together lemon peel, lemon juice and remaining ingredients. Use immediately or pour into a container with a tight-fitting lid. Cover tightly; refrigerate up to 7 days. Makes about 1 cup.

Lemon Barbecue Marinade

Delicious for poultry, beef, pork or lamb; marinate small cuts only 30 minutes or meat will toughen.

1/2 cup fresh lemon juice
1/4 cup vegetable oil or olive oil
1/2 teaspoon salt
1 garlic clove, crushed
1/2 teaspoon freshly ground black pepper

1-1/2 teaspoons finely chopped fresh thyme or
  1/2 teaspoon dried leaf thyme, crumbled
1 teaspoon Worcestershire sauce
2 tablespoons finely chopped shallots or
  green onions

In a small bowl, whisk all ingredients together. Use immediately or pour into a container with a tight-fitting lid. Cover tightly; refrigerate up to 7 days. Makes about 3/4 cup.

Orange-Glazed London Broil, page 20, with Teriyaki Marinade, and grilled zucchini slices.

Coconut-Ginger Marinade

Delicious as a pork marinade.

1/2 cup canned cream of coconut
2 tablespoons plus
 1-1/2 teaspoons soy sauce
2 tablespoons plus
 1-1/2 teaspoons fresh lemon juice

1 tablespoon plus 1-1/2 teaspoons
 finely grated fresh gingerroot
1 large garlic clove, minced
1/4 teaspoon red (cayenne) pepper

In a small bowl, whisk all ingredients together. Use immediately or pour into a container with a tight-fitting lid. Cover tightly; refrigerate up to 3 days. Makes about 3/4 cup.

Tangy Mop & Sop Sauce

A sweet-sour dipping sauce to spoon over meats and poultry or for dunking crusty bread.

1-1/2 cups cider vinegar
1 cup ketchup
1/4 teaspoon or more hot-pepper sauce

1/4 teaspoon salt
1/2 cup lightly packed brown sugar

In a medium saucepan, whisk all ingredients together. Bring to a boil, stirring occasionally. Remove sauce from heat. Taste for seasoning; add more hot-pepper sauce, if desired. Serve hot, warm or at room temperature. Use immediately or pour into a container with a tight-fitting lid. Cool then cover tightly; refrigerate up to 7 days. Makes about 2-1/2 cups.

Carolina Mop Sauce

A thin, very tangy and peppery sauce—great to brush on smoked pork or beef.

1 cup cider vinegar
1/2 cup water
2 tablespoons fresh lemon juice
3 tablespoons butter or margarine

1 teaspoon red (cayenne) pepper
2 teaspoons hot-pepper sauce
2 tablespoons Worcestershire sauce
2 tablespoons sugar

In a medium saucepan, combine all ingredients. Bring to a boil, stirring occasionally. Use immediately or pour into a container with a tight-fitting lid. Cool then cover tightly; refrigerate up to 7 days. Use to brush over smoked pork or beef every 30 minutes as it cooks or serve with smoked meats. Makes about 2 cups.

Red-Wine Marinade for Beef

Acid in the wine helps tenderize less-tender cuts of beef.

1 (1-liter) bottle dry red wine
  (about 4 cups)
1/3 cup olive oil
2 tablespoons chopped shallots or
  green onions
1/4 cup chopped celery leaves

3 large garlic cloves, minced
1/4 cup chopped fresh parsley
1 teaspoon dried leaf thyme or
  dried leaf marjoram, crumbled
1 teaspoon salt
1/2 teaspoon freshly ground black pepper

In a large bowl, whisk all ingredients together. Use immediately or pour into a container with a tight-fitting lid. Cover tightly; refrigerate up to 3 days. Makes about 5 cups.

Variation
White-Wine Marinade for Chicken: Substitute dry white wine for red wine. Marinate chicken no more than 24 hours.

East-West Barbecue Glaze

Try this piquant Oriental glaze as a table sauce for burgers, poultry and chops.

1 tablespoon cornstarch
2 tablespoons water
1 tablespoon vegetable oil
1/4 cup finely chopped onion
1-1/2 teaspoons ground ginger
2 garlic cloves, minced

1/2 cup prune juice
1/4 cup white distilled vinegar
6 tablespoons orange marmalade
1 teaspoon crushed red-pepper flakes
1/4 teaspoon salt

In a small bowl, combine cornstarch and water; set aside. Heat oil in a medium saucepan. Add onion, ginger and garlic; sauté until onion is soft. Stir in prune juice, vinegar, marmalade, red-pepper flakes and salt. Stirring constantly, bring to boil; boil 1 minute. Slowly stir cornstarch mixture into prune-juice mixture. Stirring constantly, cook until thickened, about 2 minutes. Cool slightly; serve immediately or pour into a container with a tight-fitting lid. Cover tightly; refrigerate up to 7 days. Makes about 1-1/4 cups.

Denver Brew

A zesty marinade for turkey cutlets, chicken breasts or beef cubes.

1 cup dark beer
1/4 cup vegetable oil
2 tablespoons plus 1-1/2 teaspoons
  Dijon-style mustard

2 garlic cloves, minced
1/2 teaspoon salt
1/4 teaspoon freshly ground black pepper
1/4 teaspoon sugar

In a medium bowl, whisk all ingredients together. Use immediately or pour into a container with a tight-fitting lid. Cover tightly; refrigerate up to 7 days. Makes about 1-1/3 cups.

Compound Butters

These chilled butters are delicious on fish, chicken beef, vegetables or bread. They can be refrigerated up to 2 weeks, or wrap tightly in moisture-vapor-proof wrapping and freeze up to 3 months.

Lemon-Parsley Butter

1/2 cup butter or margarine,
   room temperature
3 tablespoons finely chopped fresh parsley

1 teaspoon finely grated lemon peel
1 tablespoon fresh lemon juice
1/8 teaspoon white pepper

In a small bowl, beat butter or margarine until soft and light. Stir in remaining ingredients. Mound butter mixture on wax paper; shape into a 4-inch-long log. Wrap wax paper around log; refrigerate until firm. To serve, cut into 8 (1/2-inch-thick) slices. Makes 1/2 cup.

Variations

Lime-Cilantro Butter

1/2 cup butter or margarine,
   room temperature
1 to 2 tablespoons finely chopped
   fresh cilantro

1/2 teaspoon finely grated lime peel
1 tablespoon plus 1 teaspoon fresh lime juice
1/8 teaspoon white pepper

Mustard Butter

1/2 cup butter or margarine,
   room temperature
1 tablespoon plus 1-1/2 teaspoons
   finely chopped fresh parsley

2 teaspoons fresh lemon juice
2 tablespoons plus 1-1/2 teaspoons
   Dijon-style mustard

Butter Purees

Butter purees are more intensely flavored and colored than butter sauces. Use them warm as a basting sauce for vegetables, fish or poultry. Or let them stand at room temperature until they're spoonable and spreadable. Spread on French bread or spoon a dollop on grilled meats.

Sun-Dried-Tomato Butter Puree

1/2 cup butter or margarine

2 tablespoons chopped sun-dried tomatoes,
   packed in oil, drained

Melt butter or margarine in a small saucepan over low heat. In a blender or food processor fitted with a metal blade, process tomatoes until finely chopped. With machine running, pour in melted butter in a steady stream; process until smooth. Makes about 1/2 cup.

Gorgonzola Butter Puree

1/2 cup unsalted butter or margarine

4 oz. Gorgonzola, Roquefort or blue cheese

Melt butter or margarine in a small saucepan over low heat. In a blender or food processor fitted with a metal blade, process cheese until smooth. With machine running, pour in melted butter in a steady stream; process until smooth. Makes about 1/2 cup.

Ancho-Chile Butter Puree

2 large dried ancho chilies

1/2 cup butter or margarine

Place chilies in a medium bowl. Cover with boiling water; let stand until chilies are soft and pliable. Meanwhile, in a small saucepan, melt butter or margarine over low heat. Drain chilies; remove stems and seeds. In a blender or food processor fitted with a metal blade, process seeded chilies until finely chopped. With machine running, pour in melted butter or margarine in a steady stream; process until smooth. Makes about 2/3 cup.

How to Make Chinese Plum Sauce

1/Using back of wooden spoon, slightly mash plums to release juices. Leave seeds in plums to release more flavor.

2/Cook plums until soft. Place a strainer in a large bowl; empty plum mixture into strainer. Using a wooden spoon, press out as much liquid and pulp as possible; discard pits and skin.

Chinese Plum Sauce

Delicious on chicken or spareribs.

5 lbs. fresh red plums
1-1/4 cups sugar
1/4 cup soy sauce
2 tablespoons plus 1-1/2 teaspoons
   rice-wine vinegar

2 teaspoons sesame oil
2 large garlic cloves, minced
2 teaspoons finely grated or
   minced fresh gingerroot
1/4 teaspoon or more red (cayenne) pepper

Cut plums in half; do not pit. In a large heavy pot, combine plums and sugar. Mash plums slightly with back of a spoon to release enough juice to mix with sugar. Cover; bring to a simmer. Simmer 20 to 30 minutes until plums are very soft, stirring occasionally. Strain mixture through a sieve into a large bowl, pressing to release liquid and as much pulp as possible. Discard skins and pits. Clean pot; return puree to clean pot. Bring to a simmer; simmer until reduced to about 4 cups, stirring frequently the last 10 minutes of cooking to prevent sticking and scorching. Remove sauce from heat; stir in soy sauce, vinegar, sesame oil, garlic, gingerroot and red pepper. Use immediately, can in 1/2-pint jars or cool slightly and pour into a container with a tight-fitting lid. Cover tightly; refrigerate up to 3 weeks. **To can,** bring to a boil; ladle hot sauce into clean, hot 1/2-pint canning jars, leaving 1/2 inch headspace. Wipe rims of jars with a clean damp cloth. Close jars with metal lids and ring bands. Place in a pot or kettle of boiling water, being sure that water covers lids. Cover pot; bring water to a full boil. Begin counting processing time. At altitudes under 1000 feet, boil 20 minutes. Add 1 minute at 1000 feet; add 1 minute for each additional 1000 feet. Makes 4 cups or 4 (1/2-pint) jars.

Marge Poore's Texas Mop Sauce

A rich brown sauce, with a tangy, spicy, yet slightly sweet flavor.

1/4 cup water
1 tablespoon instant coffee granules
1 cup tomato sauce
2 tablespoons red-wine vinegar
1/2 cup Worcestershire sauce

6 tablespoons sugar
2 teaspoons dried leaf oregano, crumbled
1/4 teaspoon freshly ground black pepper
6 tablespoons butter or margarine

In a medium saucepan, bring water to a boil; stir in coffee granules until dissolved. Stir in remaining ingredients. Bring mixture to a simmer; simmer 20 minutes, stirring occasionally. Serve immediately or pour into a container with a tight-fitting lid. Cool then cover tightly; refrigerate up to 7 days. Use to brush on meats as they grill or serve with grilled meats. Makes about 2 cups.

Marge Poore's Barbecue Sauce

Less spicy and tangy than Marge Poore's Texas Mop Sauce, above. Use it on pork and beef.

1/4 cup butter or margarine
1 onion, finely chopped
3 garlic cloves, crushed
3 tablespoons lightly packed brown sugar
1/2 teaspoon Dijon-style mustard

1/2 cup peanut oil
1-1/2 cups ketchup
2/3 cup Worcestershire sauce
3 tablespoons fresh lemon juice

Melt butter or margarine in a medium saucepan. Add onion; sauté until onion is soft and slightly golden. Add garlic; sauté 1 minute longer. Stir in remaining ingredients. Bring to a simmer; simmer 25 minutes. Cover; let stand at room temperature 1 hour to let flavors blend. Serve immediately or pour into a container with a tight-fitting lid. Cover tightly; refrigerate up to 7 days. Use to brush on meats as they grill or serve with grilled meats. Makes about 3 cups.

Dry Rub for Fish

This rub is suitable for all firm-textured fish.

1 teaspoon noniodized salt
1 teaspoon freshly ground black pepper
Finely grated peel of 2 lemons
   (about 1 tablespoon)

2 tablespoons chopped fresh dill or
   2 teaspoons dill weed

In a small bowl, combine all ingredients. Use immediately or store in a container with a tight-fitting lid. Cover tightly; refrigerate up to 3 weeks. To use, rub over surface and in cavity of fish to be grilled or smoked; refrigerate 30 to 60 minutes, then cook. Makes enough rub for 2 pounds of fish.

Butter Basting Sauces

Melted butter and added seasonings make a flavorful basting sauce for vegetables, fish and poultry. They're also delicious on crusty French bread.

Mustard-Herb Butter Sauce

1/2 cup butter or margarine
2 tablespoons plus 1-1/2 teaspoons
   Dijon-style mustard
2 teaspoons fresh lemon juice
1 tablespoon plus 1-1/2 teaspoons
   finely chopped fresh parsley

1/2 to 1 teaspoon finely chopped
   fresh rosemary or 1/4 teaspoon
   dried rosemary, crumbled

Melt butter or margarine in a small saucepan over low heat. Remove pan from heat; add mustard and lemon juice. Beat with a whisk until sauce is creamy. Whisk parsley and rosemary into butter mixture. Makes about 2/3 cup.

Cilantro-Onion Butter Sauce

1/2 cup butter or margarine
2 green onions, finely chopped
2 tablespoons finely chopped fresh cilantro

1 tablespoon fresh lime juice
1/8 teaspoon red (cayenne) pepper

Melt butter or margarine in a small saucepan over low heat. Remove pan from heat; stir in remaining ingredients. Makes about 2/3 cup.

Garlic-Ginger Butter Sauce

1/2 cup butter or margarine
2 teaspoons Dijon-style mustard

2 teaspoons minced or grated fresh gingerroot
1 teaspoon minced garlic

Melt butter or margarine in a small saucepan over low heat. Remove pan from heat; stir in remaining ingredients. Makes about 1/2 cup.

Mixed-Herb Butter Sauce

1/2 cup butter or margarine
2 tablespoons mixed finely chopped
   fresh herbs or 2 teaspoons dried
   herbs, such as basil, oregano, dill,
   tarragon or sage

1 teaspoon white-wine vinegar

Melt butter or margarine in a small saucepan. Remove pan from heat; stir in herbs and vinegar. Makes about 1/2 cup.

TIP *Use basting sauces during the last 30 minutes of grilling. Then brush sauce over meat every 10 minutes until meat is browned and cooked as desired.*

Dry Rub for Pork & Lamb

Rinse the marinade off if you wish, but our preference is to leave it on.

1-1/2 tablespoons coarse salt or kosher salt
   or 1 tablespoon table salt
1 teaspoon freshly ground black pepper
1 tablespoon chopped fresh thyme or
   1 teaspoon dried leaf thyme, crumbled

2 tablespoons chopped fresh rosemary or
   2 teaspoons dried rosemary, crumbled
3 large garlic cloves, minced
1/2 teaspoon ground allspice or cloves,
   for pork only

In a small bowl, combine salt, pepper, thyme, rosemary and garlic. If dry marinade will be used for pork, add allspice or cloves. Use immediately or pour into a container with a tight-fitting lid. Cover tightly; refrigerate up to 3 weeks. To use, rub evenly over surface of meat. Place seasoned meat in a large bowl; cover and refrigerate at least 2 hours or up to 24 hours, then grill. Makes about 1/4 cup or enough dry rub for a 4-pound roast or 4 pounds of steaks or chops.

Herb Rub for Fish

You'll be pleased with the marvelous flavor result when you use this herb rub on fish.

1 tablespoon paprika
1-1/2 teaspoons finely chopped fresh
   thyme or 1/2 teaspoon dried leaf
   thyme, crumbled
1-1/2 teaspoons finely chopped fresh
   oregano or 1/2 teaspoon dried leaf
   oregano, crumbled

1 teaspoon salt
1/2 teaspoon sugar
1/4 teaspoon red (cayenne) pepper
1/4 teaspoon freshly ground black pepper

In a small bowl, combine all ingredients. Use immediately or pour into a container with a tight-fitting lid. Cover tightly; refrigerate up to 3 weeks. To use, rub evenly over surface and cavity of fish. Cover and refrigerate 30 minutes; then grill. Makes 2 to 3 tablespoons.

Herb Rub for Lamb

Marvelous flavors to complement lamb.

2 tablespoons chopped fresh rosemary or
   2 teaspoons dried rosemary, crumbled
Finely grated peel of 1 lemon
   (about 1-1/2 teaspoons)
2 teaspoons salt

1 teaspoon freshly ground black pepper
1/2 teaspoon dried leaf thyme, crumbled
1/4 teaspoon ground allspice
2 large garlic cloves, finely chopped

In a small bowl, combine rosemary, lemon peel, salt, pepper, thyme, allspice and garlic. To use, rub herb mixture over surface of lamb; cover and refrigerate at least 2 hours or up to 12 hours, then grill. Makes about 1/4 cup or enough dry rub for 3 to 4 pounds of lamb.

How to Make Salt Cure for Meat

1/In a bowl, place salt, sugar, pepper and thyme. Tear bay leaves into small pieces or crush with a mortar and pestle. Add to bowl with cloves and pepper; stir to blend. Store in a covered jar.

2/Rub the amount called for in the recipe over meat; place in bag and seal. Squeeze bag vigorously, rubbing cure into meat with your fingers.

Salt Cure for Meat

A salt cure before smoking improves the flavor of meat—but doesn't preserve the meat.

1 cup noniodized salt
3/4 cup sugar
1/4 cup freshly ground black pepper
1 teaspoon dried leaf thyme

1/2 teaspoon powdered bay leaf or
   2 large bay leaves, finely crumbled
1/2 teaspoon ground cloves
1/2 teaspoon red (cayenne) pepper

In a small bowl, combine all ingredients. Use immediately or store in a container with a tight-fitting lid. Salt cure will keep indefinitely if stored in a cool dry place. This makes enough cure for about 8 pounds of meat. Use on beef, pork, lamb or large game meats. To use, weigh meat. Using 1/4 cup cure for each pound of meat, rub cure over surface of meat. Place seasoned meat in a large heavy food-storage bag, pressing out as much air as possible; seal bag. Squeeze bag vigorously, rubbing cure into meat. Set bag in a large bowl; refrigerate 3 or 4 hours, rubbing cure into meat 2 or 3 times. Meat will begin to exude juices, forming a brine. To grill salt-cured meat, remove meat from bag; rinse well. Pat meat dry with paper towels; set on a wire rack 30 to 60 minutes to dry. Cook meat in a smoker or covered grill as directed in recipes. Makes about 2 cups.

TIP *Crack peppercorns in a mortar and pestle or by flattening them with the bottom of a heavy pan.*

Dipping Sauces

Serve these savory dipping sauces with meat, poultry, fish, vegetables and bread cubes. Whether warm or at room temperature, they add flavor and make otherwise plain dishes seem special.

Red-Chili Sauce:

1/2 cup dairy sour cream
2 tablespoons mayonnaise

1 tablespoon chili powder
1/2 teaspoon ground cumin

In a blender, combine all ingredients; process until smooth. Pour into a small dish; cover with plastic wrap or foil. Refrigerate until ready to serve, up to 5 days. Makes 2/3 cup.

Blue-Cheese Sauce:

1/2 cup dairy sour cream
1/4 cup mayonnaise
1 garlic clove, crushed
4 teaspoons milk
1-1/2 teaspoons Worcestershire sauce

1/4 teaspoon salt
Freshly ground black pepper
1-1/2 teaspoons fresh lemon juice
2 tablespoons crumbled blue cheese (1 oz.)

In a blender or food processor fitted with a metal blade, combine all ingredients; process until smooth. Pour into a small dish; cover with plastic wrap or foil. Refrigerate until ready to serve, up to 3 days. Makes 1 cup.

Cocktail Dipping Sauce

1 cup tomato-based chili sauce
2 tablespoons prepared horseradish
2 tablespoons fresh lemon juice

2 teaspoons Worcestershire sauce
1/8 to 1/4 teaspoon red (cayenne) pepper

In a small bowl, combine all ingredients. Cover with plastic wrap or foil; refrigerate at least 2 hours to let flavors blend. May be refrigerated up to 7 days. Makes about 1-1/3 cups.

Mustard-Dill Dipping Sauce

1/4 cup Dijon-style mustard
2 tablespoons white-wine vinegar
1 tablespoon or more sugar

1/2 cup finely chopped fresh dill
  or 1 tablespoon dill weed, crushed
1 cup olive oil or vegetable oil

In a small bowl, whisk together mustard, vinegar, sugar and dill. Slowly pour in oil in a steady stream, whisking until mixture is blended and thickens slightly. Cover and refrigerate at least 2 hours to let flavors blend. May be refrigerated up to 7 days. Makes about 1-1/3 cups.

Peanut Dipping Sauce

2 tablespoons butter or margarine
1/2 cup finely chopped onion
2 large garlic cloves, minced
3/4 cup chunk-style peanut butter
1 cup milk

3 tablespoons or more fresh lemon juice
2 tablespoons sugar
1 to 2 teaspoons hot-pepper sauce
2 tablespoons chopped fresh cilantro (coriander
  or Chinese parsley), if desired

Melt butter or margarine in a medium saucepan. Add onion; sauté until soft, 5 to 7 minutes. Add garlic; sauté 2 minutes longer. Whisk in peanut butter and milk, a little at a time. Stir in lemon juice; sauce will appear curdled. Bring to a boil, whisking constantly, until sauce smooths out. Stir in sugar and 1 teaspoon hot-pepper sauce. For a spicier flavor, add more hot-pepper sauce. If sauce is too sweet, add more lemon juice. Remove from heat; stir in cilantro, if desired. Serve warm or at room temperature. Use immediately or pour into a container with a tight-fitting lid. Cover tightly; refrigerate up to 3 days. Makes about 2 cups.

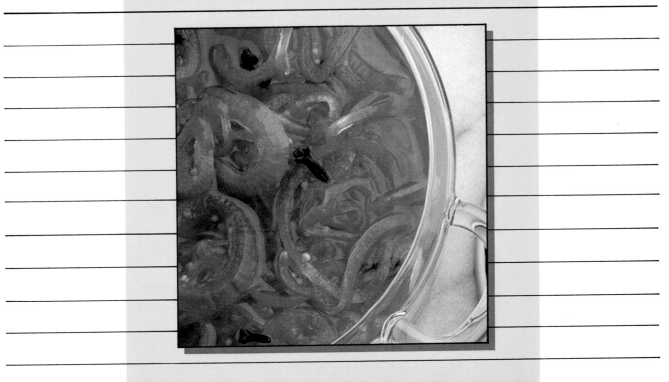

CONDIMENTS

What would a hamburger or hot dog be without mayonnaise, mustard and ketchup? Bland, to say the least! Use the following recipes or any commercial products you enjoy to spice up flavors or textures of barbecued foods.

Enjoy Aunt Louella's Watermelon Pickles, Pickled Red-Onion Rings, Dottie's Bread & Butter Pickles or Dill Pickles with any barbecued roast or ribs. If you enjoy a relish with your meal, Hot Red-Bell-Pepper Relish and Fresh-Corn Relish are sure to please.

For the time-conscious who also like to make their own condiments, Blender Mayonnaise, Coarse-Ground Mustard and Pesto Sauce will be favorites. If you are ready to put the fish on the grill and realize there is no tartar sauce, whip up our Tartar Sauce and serve it with pride. Another sauce that enhances fish is Cucumber Sauce made with fresh cucumber.

Pickled Red-Onion Rings

These easy, colorful pickles can be eaten the day they are made. Serve with hot dogs and hamburgers.

3 large red onions, thinly sliced
1-1/2 cups white distilled vinegar
1 cup sugar
1 (3-inch) cinnamon stick
1 bay leaf

10 whole cloves
1/2 teaspoon whole mustard seeds
Pinch of crushed red-pepper flakes
6 whole allspice

Place onions in a large bowl; cover with boiling water. Set aside. In a medium saucepan, combine remaining ingredients. Bring vinegar mixture to a simmer; cover and simmer 5 minutes. Meanwhile, pour onions into a colander to drain, shaking to remove excess water; return to bowl. Pour hot vinegar mixture over drained onions. Cool to room temperature; refrigerate 3 to 4 hours. Serve immediately or pour into a container with a tight-fitting lid; refrigerate up to 3 weeks. Makes about 1-1/2 quarts.

Coarse-Ground Mustard   Photos on pages 41 and 51.

Mustard seeds are located with other spices in your supermarket.

2/3 cup white-wine vinegar
1/2 cup dry white wine
1/2 cup mustard seeds
1 tablespoon honey

2 teaspoons coarse salt or kosher salt
1 garlic clove, minced
1/2 teaspoon ground allspice

In a small glass bowl, combine vinegar, wine and mustard seeds; let stand 4 hours. In a medium saucepan, combine vinegar mixture and remaining ingredients. Bring to a simmer; simmer until mixture thickens and most of liquid evaporates. Place cooked mixture in a blender or food processor fitted with a metal blade. Process with on/off motions to retain a coarse texture. Pour into a glass jar with a tight-fitting lid. Cover tightly; refrigerate up to 2 weeks. Makes about 2 cups.

Cucumber Sauce

This tangy, fresh sauce with bits of crunchy cucumber is the perfect complement to fish.

1 large cucumber
1/2 cup mayonnaise, dairy
   sour cream or combination
2 tablespoons fresh lemon juice

1/4 teaspoon salt
1/4 teaspoon freshly ground white pepper

Cut cucumber in half lengthwise; scrape out seeds. Using a sharp knife or a food processor fitted with a metal blade, finely chop seeded cucumber. In a small bowl, combine chopped cucumber, mayonnaise or sour cream, lemon juice, salt and pepper. Serve immediately or spoon into a container with a tight-fitting lid. Cover tightly; refrigerate up to 3 days. Makes about 1-1/4 cups.

Pickled Red-Onion Rings; Pesto Sauce, page 120; purchased tarragon vinegar; and Coarse-Ground Mustard.

Tomato Ketchup

This homemade ketchup is sharp, spicy and fresh tasting. Flavor improves if ketchup stands several weeks.

10 lbs. ripe regular or Italian-
   plum tomatoes, coarsely chopped
4 onions, finely chopped
2 green bell peppers, finely chopped
4 garlic cloves, finely chopped
3 celery stalks with leaves,
   finely chopped
1 (3-inch) cinnamon stick
1 teaspoon white peppercorns

1 teaspoon whole cloves
1 teaspoon whole allspice
1 teaspoon celery seeds
1 bay leaf
1 cup lightly packed dark-brown sugar
1 cup cider vinegar
2 teaspoons salt
1/4 teaspoon red (cayenne) pepper,
   if desired

In a large pot, combine tomatoes, onions, bell peppers, garlic and celery. Cover pot; bring mixture to a simmer. Simmer 40 minutes, stirring occasionally. Pour tomato mixture into a large colander set over a very large bowl or another pot. Using a large spoon or rubber spatula, press out as much juice as possible; discard pulp . Strain juice through a fine sieve into a large saucepan. You should have about 12 cups. Bring to a boil; stirring often, continue to boil until reduced to 6 cups. Tie cinnamon stick, peppercorns, cloves, allspice, celery seeds and bay leaf in a double thickness of cheesecloth or a piece of clean cotton fabric. Add to tomato mixture. Stir in brown sugar, vinegar, salt and red pepper, if desired. Cook over low heat, stirring frequently, until mixture is very thick and reduced to about 4 cups. If you like an even thicker, richer ketchup, reduce to about 3 cups. Cool; pour into a container with a tight-fitting lid. Cover tightly; refrigerate up to 4 months. **To can,** pour hot ketchup into clean, hot 1/2 pint canning jars, leaving 1/2 inch headspace. Wipe rims of jars with a clean damp cloth. Close jars with metal lids and ring bands. Place in a pot or kettle of boiling water, being sure that water covers lids. Cover pot; bring water to a full boil. Begin counting processing time. At altitudes under 1000 feet, boil 10 minutes. Add 1 minute at 1000 feet; add 1 minute for each additional 1000 feet. Makes about 4 (1/2-pint) jars.

Choddie's Mustard   Photo on page 1.

A sweet-hot mustard.

1/3 cup dry white wine
1/4 cup white-wine vinegar
1/4 cup dry mustard

1 tablespoon sugar
1/2 teaspoon salt
3 egg yolks

In a small glass bowl, combine wine, vinegar, dry mustard, sugar and salt; let stand 2 hours. In top of a double boiler, whisk egg yolks until blended; whisk in mustard mixture until smooth. Cook over simmering water, stirring constantly, until mixture thickens to the consistency of custard sauce. Cool mixture to room temperature. Pour into a container with a tight-fitting lid. Cover tightly; refrigerate up to 3 weeks. Mustard will thicken slightly as it cools; however, this is not a thick mustard. Makes about 2/3 cup.

How to Make Aunt Louella's Watermelon Pickles

1/Slice watermelon into 1-inch-thick slices for easier handling. Cut off green rind, then cut inner pink from rind. Cut remaining rind into 1-inch squares.

2/Pack hot rind into 3 sterilized jars; add 1 cinnamon stick and 1 whole clove to each jar. Fill each jar with boiling syrup, leaving a 1/2 inch headspace.

Aunt Louella's Watermelon Pickles

A traditional favorite from a favorite aunt. Flavor improves if pickles stand several weeks.

2 lbs. watermelon rind
1/2 cup noniodized salt
4 cups sugar
2 cups white distilled vinegar
2 cups water

1 lemon, thinly sliced
3 (3-inch) cinnamon sticks,
  broken in half
6 whole cloves

Remove outer green and inner pink portions from watermelon rind. Cut remaining rind into 1-inch squares. In a large bowl, combine 2 quarts water and salt, stirring until salt dissolves. Immerse rind pieces in brine; let stand in a cool place 6 hours or overnight. Drain; rinse with cold water. Drain again. Place drained rind in a large saucepan; cover with cold water. Bring to a simmer; simmer only until tender, about 10 minutes. *Do not overcook.* Drain; set aside. In same saucepan, combine sugar, vinegar, 2 cups water, lemon, cinnamon sticks and cloves. Bring to a simmer; simmer 10 minutes. Add cooked rind; simmer about 10 minutes or until rind is translucent. **To can,** pack hot rind into 3 clean, hot pint canning jars. Add 1 cinnamon piece and 1 whole clove to each jar; discard remaining cinnamon pieces and cloves. Fill each jar with boiling syrup, leaving 1/2 inch headspace. Wipe rims of jars with a clean damp cloth. Close jars with metal lids and ring bands. Place in a pot or kettle of boiling water, being sure that water covers lids. Cover pot; bring water to a full boil. Begin counting processing time. At altitudes under 1000 feet, boil 10 minutes. Add 1 minute at 1000 feet; add 1 minute for each additional 1000 feet.

Hot Red Bell-Pepper Relish

You can easily double or triple this recipe and put it up in canning jars.

4 large red bell peppers, coarsely chopped	3 tablespoons sugar
1 small onion, coarsely chopped	1/2 teaspoon salt
1/4 cup white distilled vinegar	1/8 teaspoon or more red (cayenne) pepper

Combine 1/2 of the bell peppers and 1/2 of the onion in a food processor; process with on/off motions to chop finely, leaving some texture. Repeat with remaining bell peppers and onion. In a medium saucepan, combine chopped bell-pepper mixture and remaining ingredients. Bring to a simmer; simmer, uncovered, about 15 minutes, stirring occasionally. Cool; pour into a container with a tight-fitting lid. Refrigerate up to 2 weeks. Makes about 2 cups.

Variation

To can, make a double or triple recipe. Ladle hot relish into clean, hot pint or 1/2-pint canning jars, leaving 1/4 inch headspace. Wipe rims of jars with a clean damp cloth. Close jars with metal lids and ring bands. Place in a pot or kettle of boiling water, being sure that water covers lids. Cover pot; bring water to a full boil. Begin counting processing time. At altitudes under 1000 feet, boil 20 minutes. Add 1 minute at 1000 feet; add 1 minute for each additional 1000 feet. Flavor improves if pickles stand several weeks. Makes 2 to 3 pint jars or 4 to 6 (1/2-pint) jars.

Dill Pickles

You'll find pickling salt with other canning products in your local supermarket. Flavor improves if pickles stand several weeks.

4 qts. small pickling cucumbers, not waxed, 3 to 4 inches long	9 cups water
12 to 16 large fresh dill sprigs	1 qt. white distilled vinegar (4 cups)
12 to 16 garlic cloves	3/4 cup pickling salt
	2 tablespoons sugar

Scrub cucumbers; set aside. In each of 6 to 8 clean, hot quart canning jars, place 1 dill sprig and 1 garlic clove. Pack jars, placing 6 to 8 cucumbers in each. Place another dill sprig and garlic clove in top of each jar. In a large pot, combine remaining ingredients; bring to a boil. Pour boiling vinegar mixture over cucumbers in each jar, leaving 1/2 inch headspace. Wipe rims of jars with a clean damp cloth. Close jars with metal lids and ring bands. Place in a pot or kettle of boiling water, being sure that water covers lids. Cover pot; bring water to a full boil. Begin counting processing time. At altitudes under 1000 feet, boil 15 minutes. Add 1 minute at 1000 feet; add 1 minute for each additional 1000 feet. Makes 6 to 8 quarts.

Fresh-Corn Relish

This spicy relish will keep in the refrigerator several weeks.

6 ears of fresh corn
1 cup white distilled vinegar
1/2 cup water
1 large red bell pepper, chopped
1 large green bell pepper, chopped
1 medium onion, chopped

1 cup coarsely chopped celery
1/4 cup sugar
1-1/2 teaspoons salt
1/2 teaspoon turmeric
1/2 teaspoon celery seeds
1/4 to 1/2 teaspoon crushed
   red-pepper flakes

With a sharp knife, cut corn from cobs, making 4 to 5 cups. In a large saucepan, combine corn and remaining ingredients. Bring mixture to a simmer; simmer 10 to 15 minutes. Cool slightly; pour into a large container with a tight-fitting lid. Cover tightly; refrigerate up to 2 weeks. Makes 6 cups.

Variation
Curried Corn Relish: Add 1/2 to 1 teaspoon curry powder with other seasonings.

Dottie's Bread & Butter Pickles

Crisp, sweet, old-fashioned pickle slices are perfect for munching with hamburgers. Flavor improves if pickles stand several weeks.

4 qts. thinly sliced unpeeled pickling
   cucumbers, not waxed
4 yellow onions, cut in 1/2-inch chunks
2 green bell peppers, thinly sliced
4 garlic cloves
1/3 cup pickling salt
Cracked ice

5 cups sugar
1-1/2 teaspoons ground turmeric
1-1/2 teaspoons celery seeds
2 tablespoons mustard seeds
3 cups white distilled vinegar or
   cider vinegar

In a large bowl or crock, combine cucumbers, onions, bell peppers and garlic. Add pickling salt; toss to distribute. Cover with 2 to 3 inches of cracked ice; refrigerate 8 hours or overnight. Drain vegetables thoroughly; rinse and drain again. In a very large pot, combine sugar, turmeric, celery seeds, mustard seeds and vinegar. Stir mixture over medium heat until sugar dissolves. Add cucumber mixture; increase heat to high. Bring just to a boil. **To can,** ladle pickle mixture into clean, hot pint canning jars, leaving 1/2 inch headspace. Wipe rims of jars with a clean damp cloth. Close jars with metal lids and ring bands. Place in a pot or kettle of boiling water, being sure that water covers lids. Cover pot; bring water to a full boil. Begin counting processing time. At altitudes under 1000 feet, boil 15 minutes. Add 1 minute at 1000 feet; add 1 minute for each additional 1000 feet. Makes 7 to 8 pints.

Tartar Sauce

Serve with confidence that it will be the best you've ever tasted.

1 cup mayonnaise
1/4 cup chopped cornichons or
    sour gherkins

1 tablespoon drained capers
1 tablespoon finely chopped green onion
1 tablespoon finely chopped fresh parsley

In a medium bowl, combine all ingredients; cover tightly and refrigerate 30 to 60 minutes to let flavors blend, or spoon into a container with a tight-fitting lid. Cover tightly; refrigerate up to 7 days. Makes about 1-1/4 cups.

Pesto Sauce

With pesto in the freezer, you can recapture summer at the height of winter.

3 to 4 cups loosely packed fresh
    basil leaves
4 large garlic cloves
1/2 cup pine nuts or walnuts,
    lightly toasted
3/4 cup loosely packed fresh
    parsley sprigs

1 cup olive oil
3/4 cup freshly grated Parmesan cheese
    (3 oz.)
1/2 teaspoon or more salt
1/4 teaspoon freshly ground black pepper

In a blender or food processor fitted with a metal blade, combine basil, garlic, nuts and parsley. Process with on/off motions until mixture is coarsely chopped. With processor running, add olive oil in a thin stream. Stop machine; add Parmesan cheese, 1/2 teaspoon salt and pepper. Process until as smooth as possible; add salt to taste. Pour pesto into a container with a tight-fitting lid; cover tightly. Refrigerate 2 to 3 days or freeze up to 4 months. Thaw in refrigerator or at room temperature. Makes about 2 cups.

Cheddar Topping for Burgers

A delicious and colorful topping for hamburgers.

2 cups shredded sharp Cheddar cheese
    (8 oz.)
1 (4-oz.) can chopped ripe olives
2/3 cup finely diced red bell pepper or
    1 (2-oz.) jar diced pimento, drained

3 or 4 green onions, finely chopped
1/2 cup mayonnaise
1 tablespoon plus 1-1/2 teaspoons
    prepared horseradish

Place all ingredients in a medium bowl; stir until blended. Use immediately or cover tightly and refrigerate up to 3 days. Spoon 2 to 4 teaspoons topping on each burger about 2 minutes before removing from grill. Cheese should melt slightly. Makes 3 cups.

How to Make Blender Mayonnaise

1/Place eggs, lemon juice, salt and pepper in blender container; process 10 seconds.

2/With motor still running, slowly pour in oil in a steady 1/16-inch stream. Mayonnaise will start to thicken. Immediately add water; process just until thick and smooth.

Blender Mayonnaise

If you like speed and ease of preparation, this is the mayonnaise for you!

1 egg
1 tablespoon or more fresh lemon juice
1/4 teaspoon or more salt
Pinch of white pepper

1 cup vegetable oil or 3/4 cup
   vegetable oil and 1/4 cup olive oil
1 tablespoon boiling water

In a blender, combine egg, 1 tablespoon lemon juice, 1/4 teaspoon salt and white pepper. Process 10 seconds. With blender running, add oil in a thin stream. Add water; process until thick and smooth. Taste; add more lemon juice, salt and white pepper to taste. Makes 1 cup.

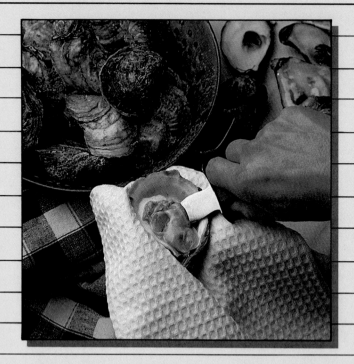

APPETIZERS

A meal always seems special if it is preceded by appetizers. Make some of your favorites, or show off your grilling expertise by preparing Crusty Bread & Cheese Brochettes, Skewered Glazed Oysters or Raclette.

Smoked-Trout & Horseradish Spread, Pesto Torte and Creamy Dill Dip are do-ahead favorites that will please any guest. Fresh Salsa & Toasted Tortillas, Mantequilla de Pobre and Grilled Quesadillas tease the appetite with Mexican spices.

Shrimp make excellent appetizers. Try your hand with Spicy Skewered Shrimp and Shrimp Sauté, both on page 96, and Shrimp Kabobs with Dipping Sauces, page 99. Other recipes that make good appetizers include Skewered Scallops & Mushrooms, page 94; Pork Saté, page 46; Faujitas, page 24; Orange-Mustard Lamb Skewers, page 62; Buffalo Wings, page 76; and any of the barbecued-rib recipes, if done with smaller baby back ribs.

Fresh Salsa & Toasted Tortillas

Try this method of baking tortilla chips. It's quick, less messy, and uses much less fat.

Fresh Salsa, see below
12 (6-inch) corn tortillas

2 to 3 tablespoons vegetable oil
Salt

Fresh Salsa:
2 cups chopped tomatoes
2 green onions with tops, chopped
2 garlic cloves, minced
1 teaspoon or more minced fresh
  jalapeño chili, serrano chili or
  canned green chilies

2 teaspoons olive oil or vegetable oil
2 teaspoons or more fresh lime juice
8 to 10 fresh cilantro sprigs, if desired,
  finely chopped
Salt

Prepare Fresh Salsa up to 3 days in advance. Preheat oven to 350F (175C). Rub both sides of each tortilla with oil; sprinkle lightly with salt. Cut each seasoned tortilla into 6 wedges; arrange in a single layer on a baking sheets. Bake in preheated oven 15 to 20 minutes or until crisp. Serve with salsa. Makes 6 to 10 appetizer servings.

Fresh Salsa:
In a medium bowl, combine tomatoes, green onions, garlic, chili peppers, oil and lime juice. Stir in cilantro, if desired; season with salt. Adjust flavors to taste, adding more chilies and lime juice, if desired. Cover with plastic wrap; refrigerate until served, up to 3 days. Makes about 2 cups.

Crusty Bread & Cheese Brochettes

Cheese, crusty bread and bits of anchovy or sun-dried tomatoes are threaded on skewers.

1 (2-oz.) can flat anchovy fillets or
  10 sun-dried tomato halves, packed in oil
1/2 cup olive oil
1/2 (1-lb.) loaf crusty French or
  Italian bread, cut in 1-inch cubes

3/4 lb. Monterey Jack cheese or
  mozzarella cheese, cut in
  1/2-inch cubes

Preheat grill; position a wire rack 4 to 6 inches from heat. Drain oil from anchovies into a large bowl or spoon 2 tablespoons oil from sun-dried tomatoes into bowl; drain anchovies or sun-dried tomato halves on paper towels. Cut anchovies into thirds or cut tomatoes into quarters; set aside. Stir olive oil into anchovy oil or tomato oil. Toss bread cubes in oil mixture until coated. Thread bread cubes, pieces of anchovy or tomatoes and cheese cubes alternately on 10 skewers. Place skewers on rack; grill 5 to 10 minutes or until bread is lightly toasted and cheese *starts* to melt, turning frequently. Serve as appetizers or with grilled meats. Makes about 25 appetizer servings.

Skewered Glazed Oysters

These are hard to beat as an appetizer, so make plenty!

Honey-Mustard Glaze, see below
9 or more small bay leaves
24 oysters, shucked

8 thin bacon slices
2 tablespoons fresh lemon juice
24 small fresh mushrooms

Honey-Mustard Glaze:
1/2 cup Dijon-style mustard
1/4 cup rice vinegar or white-wine
   vinegar
1/4 cup honey

2 tablespoons soy sauce
1 tablespoon vegetable oil
1 teaspoon sesame oil

Prepare Honey-Mustard Glaze; set aside. Soak bay leaves in warm water to cover about 10 minutes; drain and tear in half crosswise. Pat oysters dry with paper towels; set aside. In a large saucepan, bring 2 quarts water to a boil. Add bacon slices; blanch in boiling water 2 minutes. Drain and pat dry with paper towels. Cut each bacon slice in thirds. Clean saucepan; pour in another 2 quarts water and 2 tablespoons lemon juice. Bring to a boil; add mushrooms. Blanch mushrooms in boiling water 2 minutes, to prevent splitting when skewered; drain and pat dry with paper towels. Wrap each oyster with a piece of blanched bacon. On long thin metal skewers, thread bacon-wrapped oysters alternately with blanched mushrooms and soaked bay-leaf pieces. Lay skewers across a large platter or baking sheet; brush generously with glaze. Let stand 15 minutes; brush again with glaze. Let stand another 15 minutes. Preheat grill; position a wire rack 4 to 6 inches from heat. Place skewers on rack. Grill about 5 minutes or until bacon is browned on all sides, turning frequently and brushing once or twice with glaze. Remove cooked oysters and mushrooms to a warm platter; serve immediately. Makes about 12 appetizer servings.

Honey-Mustard Glaze:
Place mustard in a small saucepan; gradually whisk in remaining ingredients. Bring mixture to a simmer; simmer, partially covered, 5 minutes. Cool to room temperature. Makes about 1 cup.

Grilled Quesadillas

A quick appetizer or snack from the grill.

2 cups shredded Cheddar cheese or
   Monterey Jack cheese (8 oz.)
8 (8-inch) flour tortillas
1 large tomato, chopped
2 green onions with tops,
   sliced

1 to 3 tablespoons hot-chili salsa
2 small garlic cloves, minced
2 tablespoons finely chopped fresh
   cilantro, if desired

Preheat grill; position a wire rack 4 to 6 inches from heat. Spread 1/4 cup shredded cheese over half of each tortilla. Top each tortilla with 1/8 of each remaining ingredients. Fold tortillas over filling. Place folded tortillas on rack; grill until cheese begins to melt and tortillas brown slightly, turning once or twice. Place quesadillas on a wooden board and cut each into 3 pieces; serve immediately. Makes 8 servings.

How to Make Skewered Glazed Oysters

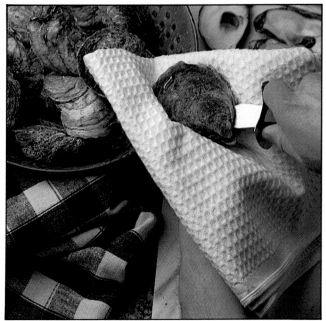

1/To shuck oysters, protect hand with a cloth towel. Place scrubbed oyster in fold of towel deep-side down. Force blade of an oyster knife between top and bottom shell opposite to hinge end of shell.

2/Pry shell open by inserting knife blade between two halves of shell. Follow contours of shell until you have severed the adductor muscle which holds shell together. Pull off top shell. Slide knife or thumb under oyster to sever bottom muscle.

Smoked-Trout & Horseradish Spread

Savor this tasty spread while dinner is on the grill. Serve as a spread for crackers and fresh vegetables, such as jícama, zucchini, cucumber and bell peppers.

3 medium smoked trout (1 to 1-1/4 lbs.)
1 (3-oz.) pkg. cream cheese,
   room temperature
1/4 cup or more whipping cream
2 to 3 teaspoons prepared horseradish
2 tablespoons fresh lemon juice
2 green onions with tops, chopped

1 tablespoon finely chopped fresh dill
   or 1 teaspoon dill weed, crumbled
Lemon slices
Parsley sprigs, if desired
Crackers
Fresh vegetables

Skin, bone and flake trout. In a blender or food processor fitted with a metal blade, puree flaked trout, cream cheese, 1/4 cup whipping cream, horseradish, lemon juice, green onions and dill. If mixture is too stiff to spread, gradually add cream until mixture is spreadable. Spoon trout mixture into a serving bowl. Cover and refrigerate until served, up to 24 hours. To serve, bring mixture to room temperature. Garnish with lemon slices and parsley, if desired. Surround with crackers and fresh vegetables. Makes about 2 cups.

Creamy Dill Dip

This creamy dip can be made in minutes. Serve with fresh vegetables or chilled cooked shrimp.

3/4 cup dairy sour cream
3/4 cup mayonnaise
1 tablespoon finely chopped green onion

2 teaspoons dill weed
1 teaspoon Beau Monde seasoning

In a medium bowl, combine all ingredients; blend well. Cover and refrigerate at least 15 minutes to let flavors blend, or refrigerate up to 3 days. Makes about 1-1/2 cups.

Mantequilla de Pobre

This literally means "poor man's butter," but is better known as "guacamole."

4 large ripe avocados, pitted, peeled
2 large tomatoes, peeled, seeded, chopped
3 tablespoons or more fresh lemon juice
2 large garlic cloves, minced

1/2 teaspoon or more salt
1/4 teaspoon freshly ground black pepper
1/8 teaspoon or more hot-pepper sauce

In a medium bowl, coarsely mash avocado with a fork. Stir in tomatoes, 3 tablespoons lemon juice, garlic, 1/2 teaspoon salt, pepper and 1/8 teaspoon hot-pepper sauce. Taste for seasoning; add more lemon juice, salt and hot-pepper sauce, if desired. Mixture should be fairly spicy. If made more than 15 minutes before serving, cover dip with plastic wrap, pressing directly on surface. Refrigerate up to 24 hours. Makes about 3 cups.

Lonnie Gandara's Crab Dip

Serve this dip warm as guests arrive and they'll be delighted. Serve hot with whole-wheat crackers, baguette slices or fresh vegetables.

1 (8-oz.) pkg. cream cheese,
   room temperature
1/2 cup dairy sour cream
1 tablespoon mayonnaise
1-1/2 teaspoons Worcestershire sauce

1/2 teaspoon dry mustard
1 cup shredded sharp Cheddar cheese (4 oz.)
1 (8-oz.) pkg. frozen crabmeat,
   thawed, flaked
1/3 cup chopped green onions with tops

Preheat oven to 350F (175C), or preheat grill or use an existing hot grill; position a wire rack 4 to 6 inches from heat. Butter a 1-quart fireproof dish; set aside. In a large bowl, beat cream cheese, sour cream and mayonnaise until smooth. Stir in Worcestershire sauce, dry mustard, Cheddar cheese, crabmeat and all but 1 tablespoon green onions. Spoon crab mixture into buttered dish. Bake in preheated oven 30 minutes or until bubbly and slightly browned. Or, set on hottest part of grill. Garnish with reserved green onions. Makes 6 to 12 appetizer servings.

Raclette

Simple and delicious—as tasty in your backyard as it is in a mountain chalet.

12 or more warm boiled new
  red potatoes
1 lb. raclette cheese, fontina cheese or
  teleme cheese

Small sweet pickles, gherkins or
  cornichons
Mustard

Preheat grill; position a wire rack 4 to 6 inches from heat. Set boiled potatoes in a pan at edge of grill to keep warm. Place cheese in a shallow enameled dish or fireproof platter. Set on hottest part of grill. After a few minutes, when cheese begins to melt and bubble, have each guest scrape a little pool of cheese onto a plate, adding a warm potato, pickle and mustard. If cheese is melting too quickly, move dish to a cooler part of grill or remove from grill. Heat of dish will keep cheese soft and runny for several minutes. Cheese must be eaten while it is hot and melted. It completely loses its charm when cold. Makes 4 servings.

Humus

A pungent mixture of pureed garbanzo beans, garlic and olive oil, to use as a dip or spread.

4 large garlic cloves
2 (15-oz.) cans garbanzo beans, drained
1/2 cup or more olive oil
1/8 teaspoon or more hot-pepper sauce

1 tablespoon or more fresh lemon juice
Salt
Freshly ground black pepper
2 tablespoons chopped fresh parsley

In a food processor fitted with a metal blade, chop garlic. Add beans; process 1 minute, stopping once or twice to scrape bowl. With processor running, slowly pour in 1/2 cup olive oil; add 1/8 teaspoon hot-pepper sauce, 1 tablespoon lemon juice and salt and pepper to taste. If mixture is too stiff to spread, gradually add olive oil until mixture is spreadable. Taste for seasoning; add more hot-pepper sauce and lemon juice, if desired. Stir in parsley. Makes about 2 cups.

Pesto Torte

It's so quick to make and always a hit; this basil-laced spread is one of our favorite appetizers. Spread on crackers, baguette slices or other party breads.

1/2 cup Pesto Sauce, page 120
1 (8-oz.) pkg. cream cheese,
  room temperature

1 cup unsalted butter, room temperature
1 fresh basil sprig, if desired

Prepare Pesto Sauce; set aside. In a medium bowl, beat cream cheese and butter until thoroughly blended. In a 2-1/2- to 3-cup crock, layer 1/3 of cream-cheese mixture; spread with 1/4 cup pesto. Repeat layering, ending with cream-cheese mixture. Cover; refrigerate up to 3 days. Remove torte from refrigerator at least 30 minutes before serving. Garnish with basil, if desired. Makes 8 to 12 servings.

VEGETABLES

Modern barbecuers are discovering there is an exciting variety of vegetables that can be grilled. We have all barbecued potatoes or corn wrapped in foil, but you'll enjoy Grilled Corn-in-the-Husk, Peppery Summer Squash, Roasted Onions, Grilled Tomatoes with Basil Vinaigrette and grilled Vegetable Brochettes.

Firm-textured vegetables, such as eggplant, potatoes, summer squash and onions, are best for slicing and grilling. Slice zucchini or crookneck squash lengthwise and eggplant, potatoes and onions crosswise to expose as much surface to the grill as possible. Cut slices uniformly thick, usually 1/3 to 1/2 inch, for even cooking. A grilling basket is a handy utensil for grilling vegetables and makes turning much easier.

Skewering vegetables will also help keep them from falling through the rack. Use a flat skewer to keep the vegetables from rolling, or use 2 water-soaked bamboo skewers. Any combination that cooks in about the same length of time can be cooked on the same skewer.

If the grill is full, bake vegetables in your oven. Corn Casserole can be prepared in the oven or on the grill.

Peppery Summer Squash   Photo on page 45.

Vegetables cut in large pieces are easier to handle on the grill.

3 tablespoons olive oil
1 tablespoon red-wine vinegar
4 medium, yellow crookneck squash,
   trimmed, cut in half lengthwise

Salt
Freshly ground black pepper

Preheat grill or use an existing hot grill; position a wire rack 4 to 6 inches from heat. In a shallow bowl or pie plate, combine olive oil and vinegar. Add squash, turning to coat. Remove from oil mixture, reserving oil mixture. Sprinkle with salt; generously sprinkle with pepper. Place squash, cut-side down, on rack. Grill 5 to 7 minutes or until tender and lightly charred, turning and brushing with reserved oil mixture. Remove to a warm platter; serve immediately. Makes 4 servings.

Zucchini with Garlic-Ginger Butter Sauce

Try some of the other butter sauces on page 109 for a different flavor treat.

1 recipe Garlic-Ginger Butter Sauce,
   page 109

8 small or 4 medium zucchini

Prepare Garlic-Ginger Butter Sauce; set aside. Preheat grill or use an existing hot grill; position a wire rack 4 to 6 inches from heat. Slice zucchini lengthwise, or slice sharply on the diagonal, making pieces big enough so they won't fall through rack. Or, to keep zucchini slices or pieces from falling through rack, place a piece of foil on rack. Use a skewer to poke 1/4-inch holes in foil to let heat and smoke penetrate zucchini. Brush zucchini with butter sauce; place seasoned zucchini on rack. Grill 10 minutes or until crisp-tender, turning and brushing lightly with butter sauce several times. Remove grilled zucchini to a platter; brush again with butter sauce. Makes 4 servings.

Roasted Onions

Roast as many onions as you need, allowing one per person.

1 recipe Lemon-Parsley Butter or
   Lime-Cilantro Butter, page 106

Medium to large onions, one per person

Prepare Lemon-Parsley Butter or Lime-Cilantro Butter; set aside. Preheat grill or use an existing hot grill; position a wire rack 4 to 6 inches from heat. Pull loose skins from onions, but do not peel or cut. Wrap each onion tightly in foil. Place foil-wrapped onions on rack; roast 1 hour or until tender when pierced with a fork. Let each person unwrap an onion, cut it into wedges and top with Lemon-Parsley Butter or Lime-Cilantro Butter. Makes 1 onion per person.

Grilled Vegetables   Photo on page 57.

Bell-pepper and onion flavors become mellow with grilling.

3 large red bell peppers
3 large green bell peppers

3 onions, cut in half crosswise
Dressing, see below

Dressing:
1/2 cup olive oil
3 tablespoons white-wine vinegar
2 tablespoons capers, drained

1 large or 2 small garlic cloves, minced
1/4 teaspoon salt
1/4 teaspoon freshly ground black pepper

Preheat grill or use an existing hot grill; position a wire rack 4 to 6 inches from heat. Using 3 long metal skewers, thread red bell peppers on 1 skewer, green bell peppers on another and onions on another. Place skewered onions on rack. Grill 15 to 20 minutes, turning occasionally. Add skewered bell peppers; grill 15 to 20 minutes longer, turning occasionally, until vegetables are charred in spots and tender when pressed. Set aside until cool enough to handle. Slide grilled vegetables off skewers. Cut grilled bell peppers into wide strips; remove seeds. Cut grilled onions into wedges. Place cut vegetables in a large serving bowl. Prepare dressing then pour over vegetables; stir to coat. Cover and let stand at room temperature at least 1 hour, or refrigerate up to 24 hours. If refrigerated, bring to room temperature before serving. Makes 6 to 10 servings.

Dressing:
In a small bowl, whisk all ingredients together. Makes about 3/4 cup.

Grilled Tomatoes with Basil Vinaigrette

Photo on page 23.

If you don't find balsamic vinegar in your local supermarket, look in a gourmet food store.

3 tablespoons olive oil
1 tablespoon balsamic vinegar or
  red-wine vinegar
1 teaspoon Dijon-style mustard

2 tablespoons finely chopped fresh
  basil or 1 to 1-1/2 teaspoons
  dried leaf basil, crumbled
3 large tomatoes

Preheat grill or use an existing hot grill; position a wire rack 4 to 6 inches from heat. In a small bowl, whisk together oil, vinegar, mustard and basil; set aside. Cut tomatoes into 1/2- to 3/4-inch-thick slices; brush with vinaigrette. Place tomatoes on rack; grill 3 to 5 minutes or until lightly browned, turning and brushing with remaining vinaigrette. Serve on a warm platter. Makes 4 to 6 servings.

Border Beans

A recipe inspired from a favorite cook and friend, Marge Poore.

1 lb. dried pinto beans
1 large ham bone
2 medium onions, chopped
3 garlic cloves, minced
2 bay leaves
1 tablespoon finely chopped fresh
  oregano or 1 teaspoon dried leaf
  oregano, crumbled
1 teaspoon or more ground cumin

2-1/2 tablespoons chili powder
1/2 teaspoon sugar
1/4 teaspoon or more crushed red-pepper
  flakes, if desired
Water
1 (16-oz.) can whole peeled tomatoes
  with juice
Salt
Freshly ground black pepper

Sort and rinse beans; place in a large pot. Cover with water. Over medium-high heat, bring to a boil; boil 2 minutes. Remove from heat; cover and let beans soak 1 hour. Discard soaking water; rinse beans with cold water. Drain. Return beans to pot with ham bone, onions, garlic, bay leaves, oregano, cumin, chili powder, sugar, red-pepper flakes and enough water to cover. Bring to a boil; reduce heat until liquid barely simmers. Simmer, partially covered, 1-1/2 to 2 hours or until beans are very tender, adding water as needed to prevent sticking and scorching. Remove and discard bay leaves. Remove ham bone; shred meat and return to pot. In a blender or food processor fitted with a metal blade, puree tomatoes and their liquid. Stir into bean mixture. Bring back to a boil, stirring occasionally. Season with salt and pepper; adjust other seasonings to taste. Beans should be thick and soft. If too soupy, uncover and cook to evaporate excess liquid. Makes 6 to 10 servings.

Charles Hall's Baked Beans

Long, slow baking gives these beans a rich, old-fashioned flavor.

4 cups dried baby lima beans or
  Great Northern beans
1/2 lb. salt pork, rind removed
2 large onions, diced
2/3 cup lightly packed dark-brown sugar
1/3 cup dark molasses

2 teaspoons dry mustard
2 teaspoons salt
1 teaspoon freshly ground black pepper
1 cup or more water
2 to 3 tablespoons ketchup

Sort and rinse beans; place in a large pot. Cover with water. Over medium-high heat, bring to a boil; boil 2 minutes. Remove from heat; cover and let beans soak 1 hour. Discard soaking water; rinse beans with cold water. Drain. Return beans to pot; cover with fresh water; bring to a boil. Reduce heat; simmer partially covered, 20 to 30 minutes or until beans are partially tender. Drain; place beans in a large bowl. Preheat oven to 250F (120C). Butter a 4-quart casserole dish or bean pot. Cut salt pork almost through at 1/2-inch intervals; set aside. Add onions, 1/3 cup brown sugar, molasses, dry mustard, salt, pepper and 1 cup water to beans, stirring until distributed. Spoon bean mixture into buttered casserole dish or bean pot; bury salt pork, cut-side down, in center of bean mixture. Cover tightly; bake 6 hours in preheated oven, adding water every 2 hours to keep beans moist. After 5 hours, stir in ketchup to taste. After 6 hours, remove cover; sprinkle beans with remaining 1/3 cup brown sugar. Bake, uncovered, 30 minutes longer. Makes 8 to 10 servings.

Grilled Corn in Bacon

If there is no room on the grill, bake corn in a preheated 350F (175C) oven 30 minutes.

8 ears of fresh corn
8 bacon slices

Freshly ground black pepper
Butter

Preheat grill or use an existing hot grill; position a wire rack 4 to 6 inches from heat. Husk corn, discarding husks and silk; brush corn with a soft brush to remove any silk that clings. Wrap a bacon slice around each husked ear of corn. Sprinkle each with pepper. Tear off 8 (12-inch) pieces of foil; wrap each ear of corn in a piece of foil, twisting ends of foil to seal. Place wrapped corn on rack. Grill over medium heat about 30 minutes, turning frequently. Remove foil; serve grilled corn with bacon and butter. Bacon will be cooked but not crisp. If you like bacon more crisp, remove from corn. Place cooked corn on edge of grill to keep warm. Place bacon on center of grill to cook a few minutes longer. Remove cooked corn to a warm platter; serve with grilled bacon. Makes 4 to 6 servings.

Grilled Onions with Butter Sauce

These will hit the spot!

1 recipe Mustard-Herb Butter Sauce,
   page 109

6 medium onions, sliced 1/2 to
   3/4-inch thick

Prepare Mustard-Herb Butter Sauce; set aside. Preheat grill or use an existing hot grill; position a wire rack 4 to 6 inches from heat. To keep onions from falling through rack, place a piece of foil on rack. Use a skewer to poke 1/4-inch holes in foil to let heat and smoke penetrate onions. Brush onions with butter sauce; place seasoned onions on foil. Grill 10 to 12 minutes or until tender, turning and brushing with butter sauce several times. Removed grilled onions to a platter; brush with butter sauce. Makes 6 to 8 servings.

Eggplant with Cilantro-Onion Butter

To make a mixed vegetable grill, serve with Grilled Vegetables, page 130.

1 recipe Cilantro-Onion Butter Sauce,
   page 109
1 medium eggplant (1 to 1-1/4 lbs.),
   trimmed, cut in 1/4-inch-thick slices

Salt

Prepare Cilantro-Onion Butter Sauce; set aside. Preheat grill or use an existing hot grill; position a wire rack 4 to 6 inches from heat. Sprinkle eggplant slices with salt, then brush with butter sauce. Place seasoned eggplant slices on rack; grill 10 minutes or until lightly browned, turning and brushing lightly with butter sauce several time. Remove grilled eggplant to a platter; brush with butter sauce. Makes 5 to 6 servings.

How to Make Potatoes Baked in Coals

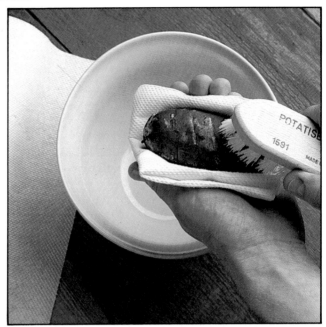

1/With long-handled tongs, arrange hot coals on bottom grill. Make 6 to 8 pockets or indentations, each large enough to hold a potato. Using tongs, place a potato into each indentation.

2/After cooking, lift potatoes from coals using tongs. Place a potato in a towel or cloth to protect hands. Using a stiff brush, brush skin that was in direct contact with coals. Skin that is charred is not edible.

Potatoes Baked in Coals

Bake in very low-glowing coals to get a thick, crackling skin and a soft; mealy inside.

6 to 8 large baking potatoes,
   sweet potatoes, yams or combination
Salt
Freshly ground black pepper

Butter or margarine
Sour cream, if desired
Lemon wedges, if desired

Preheat grill; let coals burn down until low-glowing, or use an existing hot grill. Scrub potatoes; prick each potato several times with a fork. With tongs arrange hot coals into 6 to 8 pockets or indentations, each large enough to hold a potato. Place a potato in each pocket; cover grill. Cook 30 minutes or until potatoes are easily pierced with a fork or knife. Using long-handled tongs, lift cooked potatoes from coals. Holding each potato with an oven mitt, scrape skin with a stiff brush. Skin that was in direct contact with coals will be charred and not edible. Place potatoes on a platter, blackened-side down; cut an **X** in top of each potato. Press from both ends to open up slightly. Sprinkle with salt and pepper. Serve with butter or margarine, sour cream and lemon wedges, if desired. Makes 6 to 8 servings.

Variation
Potatoes Baked Over Coals: Position a wire rack 4 to 6 inches from heat; place scrubbed and pierced potatoes on rack. Cover grill; cook 1 hour and 15 minutes to 2 hours, depending on how hot coals are. Potatoes are done when easily pierced with a fork or knife. It's difficult to overbake them, although the longer they bake the more crackly the skins become.

Vegetable Brochettes   Photos on cover and opposite.

Colorful, skewered vegetables are first marinated in an anchovy vinaigrette.

3 large zucchini, cut in
   3/4-inch-thick slices
2 red or green bell peppers,
   cut in 1-1/2-inch squares

8 (3-inch-long) green onions
1 medium eggplant (about 3/4 lb.),
   cut into 1-1/2-inch cubes
Anchovy Vinaigrette, see below

Anchovy Vinaigrette:
1 tablespoon anchovy paste
1 garlic clove, minced

2 tablespoons red-wine vinegar
1/4 cup olive oil

Bring a large pan of water to a boil. Add zucchini, bell peppers, green onions and eggplant; cook 2 minutes. Drain cooked vegetables in a colander; rinse with cold water to stop cooking. Let stand 4 to 5 minutes, shaking occasionally to remove excess moisture, then drain on paper towels. Prepare Anchovy Vinaigrette; add blanched vegetables. Toss to coat; let stand about 30 minutes, tossing occasionally. Preheat grill or use an existing hot grill; position a wire rack 4 to 6 inches from heat. Drain vegetables, reserving marinade. Thread drained vegetables alternately onto 4 long metal skewers, beginning and ending with zucchini. Place skewered vegetables on rack. Grill about 12 minutes or until lightly browned and slightly crisp-tender, turning frequently and brushing 2 or 3 times with reserved marinade. To serve, arrange brochettes on a platter. Makes 4 servings.

Anchovy Vinaigrette:
In a large bowl, whisk all ingredients together. Makes about 1/2 cup.

Pesto Tomatoes   Photo on page 17.

Delicious when tomatoes are at the peak of their season.

Fresh Pesto, see below
Lettuce leaves

4 medium tomatoes
Freshly ground black pepper

Fresh Pesto:
1/3 cup tightly packed fresh
   basil leaves
1/3 cup olive oil or vegetable oil or
   combination
3 tablespoons freshly grated Parmesan
   cheese

1 tablespoon red-wine vinegar
1/4 teaspoon minced garlic
1/4 teaspoon salt
1/4 teaspoon sugar

Prepare Fresh Pesto; set aside. Line a platter with lettuce leaves. Core tomatoes; cut in slices or wedges. Arrange on lettuce-lined platter. Spoon pesto over sliced tomatoes; sprinkle with pepper to taste. Makes 6 to 8 servings.

Fresh Pesto:
In a blender or food processor fitted with a metal blade, combine all ingredients; process until as smooth as possible. Makes about 1/2 cup.

Vegetable Brochettes; Garbanzo, Feta & Olive Salad, page 142; and Tabbouleh Salad, page 145.

Skewered Potatoes   Photo on page 41.

Steamy potatoes with crisp, brown skins are a wonderful accompaniment to barbecued meats.

18 to 20 small, white- or red-skinned,
  new potatoes (about 2 lbs.)
Salt
1/2 cup butter or margarine

2 tablespoons chopped fresh parsley
1 tablespoon finely chopped fresh
  rosemary or 1-1/2 teaspoons dried
  rosemary, if desired, crumbled
Freshly ground black pepper

Cook potatoes in lightly salted boiling water 10 to 15 minutes or until barely tender when pierced with a fork; drain. Immerse in cold water to stop cooking; drain well. Preheat grill or use an existing hot grill; position a wire rack 4 to 6 inches from heat. Thread potatoes on 5 metal skewers. In a small saucepan, melt butter or margarine; stir in parsley and rosemary, if desired. Brush potatoes lightly with butter mixture; place skewered potatoes on rack. Sprinkle with salt and pepper. Grill 8 to 10 minutes or until skins are well-browned, turning frequently and brushing occasionally with butter mixture. To serve, arrange grilled potatoes on a platter. Makes 6 servings.

John's Doctored Sauerkraut   Photo on page 51.

Serve this sauerkraut with Mixed-Sausage Grill, page 50, and plenty of mustard.

1 (27-oz.) can sauerkraut
1-1/2 cups beer, beef stock or
  chicken stock

4 juniper berries
1 bay leaf
5 black peppercorns

Pour sauerkraut into a colander to drain. Rinse thoroughly with cold water; press out as much liquid as possible. In a medium saucepan, combine rinsed sauerkraut and beer or stock. Add juniper berries, bay leaf and peppercorns. Bring to a simmer; simmer over low heat 30 to 40 minutes. Drain off most of liquid; remove and discard bay leaf. Makes 4 to 6 servings.

Grilled Potato Slices

Crisp, golden brown potato slices are the perfect complement to many grilled meats.

About 1-1/2 lbs. white- or red-skinned
  potatoes, sweet potatoes or yams
Salt
1/3 cup butter or margarine
1-1/2 tablespoons chopped fresh parsley

2 teaspoons finely chopped fresh
  rosemary or 1 teaspoon dried
  rosemary, if desired, crumbled
Freshly ground black pepper

Cook potatoes in lightly salted boiling water 10 to 15 minutes or until barely tender when pierced with a fork; drain. Immerse in cold water to stop cooking; drain well. Preheat grill or use an existing hot grill; position a wire rack 4 to 6 inches from heat. In a small saucepan, melt butter or margarine; stir in parsley and rosemary, if desired. Keep warm. Cut cooled potatoes into 1-inch-thick slices. Brush both sides of each potato slice with butter mixture; sprinkle with salt and pepper. Place seasoned potato slices on rack. Grill about 12 minutes or until tender and well-browned on both sides, turning occasionally and brushing 2 or 3 times with butter mixture. To serve, arrange grilled potato slices on a platter. Makes 4 servings.

How to Make Grilled Corn-in-the-Husk

1/Carefully peel back husks. Pull off silk; brush corn kernels with soft butter and sprinkle with salt. Push husks back over cob; tie tips closed with string.

2/Grill corn, turning often, until husks are evenly darkened and blackened in spots. To serve, remove husks, brush with more butter.

Grilled Corn-in-the-Husk   Photos on cover and page 45.

Grilling seems to highlight the flavor of sweet, fresh corn. Enjoy it hot from the fire.

8 ears of fresh corn, in husks   **Salt**
1/4 cup butter or margarine, melted

Preheat grill or use an existing hot grill; position a wire rack 4 to 6 inches from heat. Carefully peel back husks on each ear of corn; remove and discard silk. Brush kernels with a soft brush to remove any silk that clings. Brush corn lightly with butter or margarine; sprinkle with salt. Pull husks back up around corn; tie tops closed with heavy string. Place wrapped corn on grill. Grill about 12 minutes or until husks are evenly darkened and blackened in spots, turning often. To serve, cut off strings; remove husks from corn. Makes 8 servings.

Marinated Vegetable Plate   Photo on page 75.

Choose any combination of vegetables to create this colorful arranged salad.

1/2 cup olive oil or vegetable oil
  or combination
3 tablespoons white-wine vinegar
1 tablespoon Dijon-style mustard
1 to 2 teaspoons finely chopped fresh
  oregano or tarragon or 1/2 teaspoon
  dried leaf oregano or tarragon,
  crumbled

16 to 20 cherry tomatoes, halved
2 small zucchini, cut in 1/8-inch slices
8 oz. jícama, peeled, cut in
  2" x 1/4" strips
Romaine-lettuce leaves

In a medium bowl, whisk together oil, vinegar, mustard and oregano or tarragon. Dividing evenly, pour dressing into 3 small bowls. Add tomatoes to one, zucchini to another and jícama to third. Cover and let vegetables stand in dressing at room temperature at least 10 minutes or up to 30 minutes. Line a platter with romaine-lettuce leaves. Lift vegetables from dressing; arrange in strips on lettuce-lined platter. Makes 4 to 6 servings.

Variation
Any combination of fresh vegetables can be used, such as red- or green-bell-pepper strips, tomato wedges, cold cubed cooked potatoes, blanched baby turnips, blanched green beans, edible pea pods or blanched sliced carrots.

Corn Casserole

This delicious dish is similar to Southern corn pudding.

3 large ears of fresh corn or
  2 (16-oz.) cans whole-kernel corn,
  drained
1/2 cup yellow cornmeal
1/2 cup all-purpose flour
1 teaspoon salt
1 tablespoon baking powder

1/2 teaspoon baking soda
1/2 pint dairy sour cream (1 cup)
1/4 cup butter or margarine, melted, cooled
2 eggs, slightly beaten
1/2 cup shredded Cheddar cheese or
  Swiss cheese (2 oz.)
1 (4-oz.) can diced green chilies

Prepare grill or use an existing grill; position rack 4 to 6 inches from heat. Grease a 10- or 11-inch cast-iron skillet; set aside. With a sharp knife, cut corn from cobs, measure out 2 cups. Reserve any remaining corn for another purpose. In a medium bowl, combine cornmeal, flour, salt, baking powder and baking soda; stir in corn. In another medium bowl, combine sour cream, butter or margarine, eggs, cheese and chilies. Pour sour-cream mixture over dry ingredients; stir only until dry ingredients are moistened. Do not overmix. Spread batter evenly in buttered skillet; place on hottest part of grill. Cover grill; cook 30 to 45 minutes or until top is golden and a wooden pick inserted in center comes out clean. Makes 4 to 6 servings.

Variation
Oven-Baked Corn Casserole: Preheat oven to 350F (175C). Butter a 9" x 7" casserole dish. Prepare corn mixture; spoon into buttered casserole. Bake in preheated oven 30 minutes or until top is golden and a wooden pick inserted in center comes out clean.

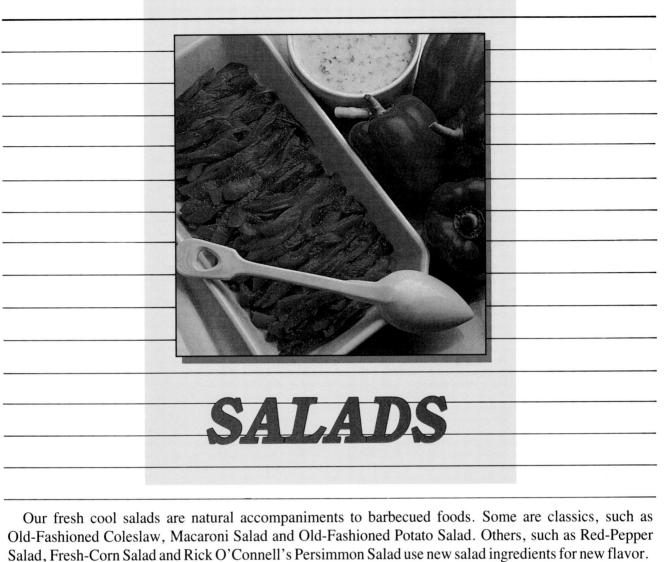

SALADS

Our fresh cool salads are natural accompaniments to barbecued foods. Some are classics, such as Old-Fashioned Coleslaw, Macaroni Salad and Old-Fashioned Potato Salad. Others, such as Red-Pepper Salad, Fresh-Corn Salad and Rick O'Connell's Persimmon Salad use new salad ingredients for new flavor.

Leftover grilled meats make excellent salad ingredients. Shredded or cubed grilled poultry make a tasty salad, or try adding pieces of cubed barbecued beef or pork to a hearty potato salad. Garnish with slices of tomato and onion. The smoky flavor of the meat will give an elusive and intriguing taste.

After they have been grilled and cooled completely, Butterflied Squab, page 72, makes delicious cold leftovers or picnic food the next day, served with mayonnaise and Rice Salad with Mustard Vinaigrette or Old-Fashioned Potato Salad.

Petite-Pea Salad

This is a colorful, simple salad—perfect for a buffet.

Pinch of sugar
4 cups fresh shelled tiny peas or
  2 (10-oz.) pkgs. frozen tiny peas, thawed
2 tablespoons mayonnaise
2 tablespoons dairy sour cream

2 teaspoons fresh lemon juice
1 to 2 tablespoons finely chopped fresh
  dill or 3/4 to 1 teaspoon dill weed,
  crumbled
2 to 3 teaspoons chopped chives, if desired

If using fresh peas, bring 2 quarts water and a pinch of sugar to a boil. Add fresh peas, cook 5 to 7 minutes until tender; remove from heat and drain. Rinse peas under cold running water; drain again and pat dry with paper towels. If using frozen peas, pat dry with paper towels. Place peas in a large serving bowl. In a small bowl, combine mayonnaise, sour cream, lemon juice, dill and chives, if desired. Just before serving, add dressing to peas, tossing to coat. Makes 6 to 8 servings.

Macaroni Salad

An old-fashioned favorite that's standard fare at picnics and backyard barbecues.

1 (8-oz.) pkg. elbow, shell or
  salad macaroni (2 cups)
Salt
1 cup thinly sliced celery
1 (2-1/4-oz.) can chopped ripe olives
1/2 cup chopped green onions
1/4 cup finely chopped fresh parsley

1/2 cup chopped green or red bell pepper
1 cup mayonnaise
2 tablespoons cider vinegar or
  white-wine vinegar
Freshly ground black pepper
2 hard-cooked eggs, sliced
Parsley sprigs or watercress sprigs

Cook macaroni in lightly salted boiling water until al dente or just tender to the bite. Drain; rinse with cold water, then drain again. In a large bowl, combine drained macaroni, celery, olives, green onions, chopped parsley and bell pepper. In a small bowl, combine mayonnaise, vinegar, 1/2 teaspoon salt and black pepper. Pour over macaroni mixture; toss to coat. Cover and refrigerate 3 to 4 hours to let flavors blend. To serve, spoon salad into a large serving bowl. Garnish with egg slices and parsley sprigs or watercress sprigs. Makes 6 to 8 servings.

How to Make Bell-Pepper Salad

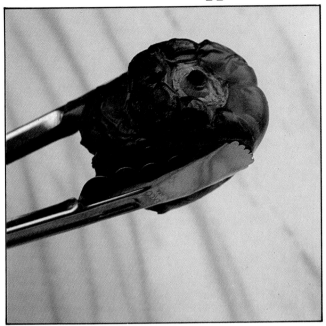

1/Place peppers under a broiler; broil, turning often, until peppers are charred and puffy all over. Let stand until cool enough to handle. With your fingers, peel off skin.

2/Do not rinse peeled peppers or flavor will be lost. Cut peppers into 1/4-inch strips; place in a shallow dish. Pour vinaigrette over peppers and marinade.

Bell-Pepper Salad

A colorful, zesty salad.

1/4 cup red-wine vinegar or
   3 tablespoons balsamic vinegar
6 tablespoons Dijon-style mustard
1/2 cup olive oil
1/2 teaspoon salt
1/4 teaspoon freshly ground pepper
3 or 4 drops hot-pepper sauce,
   if desired

1/4 cup chopped fresh basil, chives or
   parsley, or 1/4 cup chopped fresh
   parsley and 1 teaspoon dried leaf
   basil or tarragon, crumbled
12 large red bell peppers (green or
   yellow, or a combination)

In a medium bowl, combine vinegar and mustard, beating with a whisk until smooth. Slowly whisk in olive oil; mixture will look like mayonnaise. Stir in salt, pepper and a few drops of hot-pepper sauce, if desired. Stir in herbs, cover and refrigerate 2 to 4 hours. Preheat broiler. Line a large, shallow baking pan or baking sheet with foil to make clean-up easier. Place bell peppers in a single layer in pan; place 2 to 4 inches under broiler. Broil until peppers are blistered on all sides, turning often with long-handled tongs. When peppers are charred and puffed all over, remove from broiler. Let stand at room temperature until cool enough to handle; strip off peel with your fingers or tip of a knife. Do not rinse peeled peppers or flavor will be lost. Cut peeled peppers into 1/4-inch strips; set aside. Cover and refrigerate peppers. Remove peppers 30 minutes before serving. Serve at room temperature with dressing spooned over top. Makes 6 to 8 servings.

Old-Fashioned Potato Salad   Photo on page 69.

A traditional potato salad with potatoes, onion, celery and a creamy dressing goes well with any barbecued meat or poultry.

3 lbs. (about 8 medium) white- or
   red-skinned potatoes
Salt
3 tablespoons red-wine vinegar
1/4 cup vegetable oil
1/2 teaspoon or more freshly ground
   pepper
1/4 cup chopped fresh parsley

1/2 cup diced celery
1/2 cup chopped red onion or green
   onions
1/4 cup diced sweet pickle
4 hard-cooked eggs, 3 chopped, 1 sliced
1/3 to 1/2 cup mayonnaise or more
Parsley sprigs

Cook potatoes in lightly salted boiling water 20 to 30 minutes or until tender when pierced. Meanwhile, in a small bowl, combine vinegar, oil, 1/2 teaspoon salt, 1/2 teaspoon pepper and chopped parsley; set aside. Drain cooked potatoes; when cool enough to handle, cut potatoes into 1/4-inch-thick slices. Place potato slices in a large bowl. Add vinegar mixture; toss to coat potato slices. Cool to room temperature. Add celery, red or green onions, pickle and chopped eggs; toss again. Gently fold in mayonnaise, coating all ingredients. Add more mayonnaise, salt and pepper, if desired. Cover and refrigerate several hours or overnight before serving. Season to taste with salt. Mound salad in a large serving bowl; garnish with parsley sprigs and sliced egg. Makes 6 to 8 servings.

Garbanzo, Feta & Olive Salad   Photo on page 135.

Greek flavors blend beautifully in a rich bean salad.

1 (15-1/2-oz.) can garbanzo beans,
   drained
1/2 cup crumbled feta cheese
   (about 3 oz.)
1/3 cup ripe-olive slices or wedges
1 large tomato, seeded, diced
2 green onions with tops, sliced
2 tablespoons finely chopped
   fresh parsley

2 tablespoons olive oil
2 tablespoons red-wine vinegar
Salt
Freshly ground black pepper
1/2 to 1 teaspoon finely chopped
   fresh oregano, if desired
1/2 to 1 teaspoon finely chopped
   fresh rosemary, if desired

In a large bowl, combine garbanzo beans, feta cheese, olives, tomato, onions and parsley. In a small bowl, whisk together olive oil and vinegar. Pour over salad; tossing to distribute. Season to taste with salt and pepper. Stir in oregano and rosemary, if desired. Makes 4 to 6 servings.

Rick O'Connell's Persimmon Salad

Fu Yu persimmons are edible and sweet while still firm.

1/2 cup olive oil
1 cup pecan halves or large pecan pieces
2 to 3 tablespoons red-wine vinegar,
    sherry vinegar or raspberry-flavored
    vinegar
1/4 teaspoon salt
1/4 teaspoon freshly ground black pepper

3 Belgian endive
6 persimmons
1 (2- to 3-oz.) bunch watercress,
    large stems removed
2 fresh fennel stalks, cut in slivers
    2 to 3 inches long, 1/8 inch wide

In a small skillet, heat 2 tablespoons olive oil over medium-high heat. Add pecans; sauté 1 to 2 minutes until lightly toasted. Pour into a small bowl; set aside. In another small bowl, whisk together remaining 6 tablespoons olive oil, 2 tablespoons vinegar, salt and pepper. Dressing should be slightly tart because persimmons are very sweet; add more vinegar, if desired. Cut each endive in half lengthwise; cut diagonally into 1-inch pieces. Scatter pieces evenly on a large platter. Remove stems from persimmons; cut fruit in 1/4-inch-thick slices. Lay slices over endive pieces, overlapping slightly if necessary. Scatter watercress sprigs and fennel slivers over top. Sprinkle with toasted pecans; drizzle dressing over salad. Makes 6 to 8 servings.

Tortellini Salad Photo on page 85.

The strong-flavored Mustard-Basil Vinaigrette makes this pasta salad special.

1 (7-oz.) pkg. dried cheese-filled
    tortellini
Mustard-Basil Vinaigrette, see below
1/2 cup freshly grated Asiago, Romano
    or Parmesan cheese (1-1/2 oz.)
1 large tomato, chopped

2 oz. fresh edible pea pods, blanched,
    cut diagonally into 1-1/4-inch pieces
    (about 1 cup)
Salt
Freshly ground black pepper

Mustard-Basil Vinaigrette:
1/2 cup olive oil
3 tablespoons white-wine vinegar
2-1/2 tablespoons Dijon-style mustard
3 tablespoons or more finely chopped
    fresh basil or dill or 3/4 to
    1 teaspoon dried leaf basil or
    dill weed, crumbled

2 tablespoons finely chopped shallots
    or green onions
1 large garlic clove, minced
1/2 teaspoon sugar

Cook tortellini according to package directions. Drain; rinse with cold water then drain again. Cool to room temperature or cover and refrigerate cooked tortellini until chilled. Prepare Mustard-Basil Vinaigrette. In a large bowl, combine cooled cooked tortellini, cheese, tomato and pea pods. Add vinaigrette; gently toss to coat evenly. Season with salt and pepper to taste. Cover and let stand at least 30 minutes before serving to let flavors blend. Serve at room temperature. Makes 6 to 10 servings.

Mustard-Basil Vinaigrette:
In a small bowl, whisk all ingredients together. Makes about 3/4 cup.

Southwest Bean Salad with Chili Vinaigrette

The piquantness of bottled chili salsa varies, so taste before adding the whole amount.

Chili Vinaigrette, see below
Sour Cream Topping, see below
1 (16-oz.) can black beans
1 (15-oz.) can kidney beans

1 (15-oz.) can pinto beans
2 medium tomatoes, seeded, coarsely chopped
1 cup sliced green onions with tops
1/2 cup diced celery

Chili Vinaigrette:
6 tablespoons vegetable oil
3 to 6 tablespoons bottled chili salsa

3 tablespoons red-wine vinegar
1/2 to 3/4 teaspoon ground cumin

Sour Cream Topping:
3/4 cup dairy sour cream
1 tablespoon chopped cilantro

Prepare Chili Vinaigrette and Sour Cream Topping; refrigerate until served. Drain all beans into a colander; rinse and drain again. In a large bowl, combine drained beans, tomatoes, green onions and celery. Add Chili Vinaigrette; gently toss to coat bean mixture. Cover and refrigerate up to 24 hours. Top each serving with a dollop of Sour Cream Topping, or serve topping separately. Makes 6 to 10 servings.

Chili Vinaigrette:

In a small bowl, whisk all ingredients together. Refrigerate until served. Makes about 3/4 cup.

Sour-Cream Topping:

In a small bowl, combine sour cream and cilantro. Refrigerate until served. Makes 3/4 cup.

Old-Fashioned Coleslaw

A very simple slaw with a slightly sweet-sour flavor.

1 small head cabbage (about 3/4 pound)
2 tablespoons sugar
1/2 teaspoon salt
1 large carrot, grated

1/2 cup mayonnaise
2 tablespoons cider vinegar
2 tablespoons chopped fresh parsley

Cut cabbage in quarters; remove core. Shred cabbage; place in a large bowl. Sprinkle with sugar and salt; toss to coat. Let stand about 15 minutes until cabbage has wilted slightly; drain off any juice that forms. Add carrot; toss to distribute. In a small bowl, combine mayonnaise and vinegar; stir into cabbage mixture. Cover salad and refrigerate until chilled. Sprinkle with parsley before serving. Makes 4 to 5 servings.

Variation

Add 1 grated tart green apple with carrot. This variation is especially good served with pork.

Tabbouleh   Photo on page 135.

A fresh, nutritious salad from the Middle East.

3/4 cup bulgur or cracked wheat
1-1/2 cups chopped fresh parsley
3 medium tomatoes, seeded, chopped
1/2 cup coarsely chopped green onions
  with tops
3 tablespoons finely chopped fresh mint or
  2 teaspoons dry mint leaves, crumbled

1/2 cup olive oil or vegetable oil
1/4 cup fresh lemon juice
Salt
Freshly ground black pepper
8 to 10 Greek olives or ripe olives

If using bulgur, in a medium bowl, combine bulgur and 2 cups boiling water; let stand 1 hour. Drain; then squeeze 1 handful of bulgur at a time in a clean towel to remove as much water as possible. Return drained bulgur to bowl. Add parsley, tomatoes, green onions and mint; toss. In a small bowl, whisk together oil and lemon juice. Pour over salad; toss to coat. Season to taste with salt and pepper. Cover; refrigerate at least 1 hour. Toss just before serving. Garnish with olives. Makes 4 to 6 servings.

Variation
Add 1 cup fresh or cold, cooked vegetables or 1/2 cup chopped ham.

Fresh-Corn Salad   Photo on page 69.

A colorful, summer salad with a slightly crunchy texture.

Vinaigrette Dressing, see below
6 large ears of fresh corn
1/2 cup diced green bell pepper
1/2 cup diced red bell pepper

2 tablespoons capers, drained
1/2 cup diced celery
1/4 cup chopped green onions
1/4 cup finely chopped fresh parsley

Vinaigrette Dressing:
3 tablespoons cider vinegar
1 tablespoon Dijon-style mustard
1/3 cup olive oil or vegetable oil
1 teaspoon sugar

1/2 teaspoon salt
1/2 teaspoon freshly ground black pepper
Dash of hot-pepper sauce

Prepare Vinaigrette Dressing; set aside. With a sharp knife, cut corn from cobs, making 4 to 5 cups. In a large bowl, combine corn, bell peppers, capers, celery, green onions and parsley. Pour dressing over top; toss to coat. Cover and refrigerate about 1 hour, tossing once or twice. Makes 6 to 8 servings.

Vinaigrette Dressing:
In a small bowl, whisk together vinegar and mustard until blended. Whisk in remaining ingredients. Makes about 1/2 cup.

Rice Salad with Mustard Vinaigrette

Photo on page 63.

A colorful, refreshing, yet substantial salad that allows for a number of variations.

1-1/3 cups raw-white long-grain rice
2-1/2 cups water
Mustard Vinaigrette, see below
3 tablespoons olive oil
1/2 cup chopped red bell pepper
1/2 cup chopped green bell pepper
1/2 cup chopped yellow bell pepper or
 additional red or green bell pepper
1 large tomato, diced

1 Red Delicious apple, diced
1/2 cup chopped green onions,
 including tops
1/4 cup chopped fresh parsley
1 (4-1/2-oz.) can chopped ripe olives
1/4 cup pine nuts or chopped walnuts,
 toasted
Salt, if desired
Freshly ground black pepper, if desired

Mustard Vinaigrette:
1/2 cup olive oil
2 to 3 tablespoons red-wine vinegar
1 garlic clove, minced
1/2 teaspoon salt
1/2 teaspoon freshly ground black pepper

1 tablespoon Dijon-style mustard
1 tablespoon chopped fresh tarragon or
 1/2 teaspoon dried leaf tarragon,
 crumbled

Place water in a 3-quart saucepan; stir in rice. Bring to a boil over high heat; cover pan, reduce heat and simmer 20 minutes or until liquid is absorbed. Remove from heat; cool to lukewarm. Meanwhile, prepare Mustard Vinaigrette; refrigerate at least 1 hour before using. In a large bowl, toss warm rice with olive oil; cool to room temperature. Add bell peppers, tomato, apple, green onions, parsley, olives and nuts; toss to distribute. Drizzle vinaigrette over top; toss to coat all ingredients. Season with salt and pepper, if desired. Mound salad in a large serving bowl or on a platter; serve at room temperature. To make ahead, cover salad and refrigerate up to 4 hours. To serve, bring to room temperature. Makes 8 servings.

Mustard Vinaigrette:
In a container with a tight-fitting lid, combine all ingredients. Cover tightly; shake vigorously until dressing is blended. Makes about 3/4 cup.

Variation
Add 1 cup diced cooked chicken, diced cooked roast beef, tiny shrimp, flaked crabmeat or cooked and chilled tiny green peas.

BREADS

Bake Cornmeal-Cinnamon-Raisin Bread on the grill while a large piece of meat is roasting. Or after the meat is cooked, pop Skillet-Grilled Buttermilk Biscuits into a cast-iron skillet and bake on the grill until puffed and golden. Everyone will know you are a skilled barbecuer when you can grill bread!

Store-bought breads are excellent with barbecues when topped with a buttery garlic mixture or sliced and stuffed with a garlic-cheese mixture. Try Gayle's Soft & Buttery Garlic Bread or Foil-Wrapped Garlic-Cheese Bread for starters.

If the grill is full and you want the bread done ahead, bake Cornmeal-Pecan Muffins in your oven. Grill-Baked Corn Bread can also be done in the oven as a loaf or as muffins.

When baking on the grill, place one pan inside another for insulation. Stacking two pans together—they need not fit perfectly—prevents burned bread bottoms. Generously grease the top pan before adding the batter or bread dough.

Cornmeal-Cinnamon-Raisin Bread

A crusty loaf, slightly sweet and spicy with cinnamon. Toast and serve with cream cheese.

2-1/2 cups boiling water
1 cup raisins
2/3 cup nonfat dry milk powder
6 tablespoons butter or margarine,
  room temperature
1/2 cup sugar

2 teaspoons salt
2 (1/4-oz.) pkgs. active dry yeast
  (about 5 teaspoons)
1 cup yellow or white cornmeal
2 teaspoons ground cinnamon
5-1/2 to 6 cups all-purpose flour

In a large bowl, combine boiling water, raisins, dry milk powder, butter or margarine, sugar and salt. Let stand until 110F (45C). Sprinkle yeast over warm mixture; stir in. Let stand 5 to 10 minutes or until foamy. Stir in cornmeal, cinnamon and 3 cups flour. Beat vigorously 1 to 2 minutes. Add enough remaining flour to make a lukewarm dough that comes away from side of bowl. Turn out onto a lightly floured surface; knead 1 to 2 minutes, cover and let rest 10 minutes. Clean and grease bowl; grease 2 round 8- or 9-inch baking pans. Set aside. Knead dough 10 minutes longer or until dough is smooth and elastic, adding only enough flour so dough is not sticky. Place in greased bowl, turning to grease all sides. Cover with a dry cloth. Let rise in a warm place, free from drafts, 1 hour or until doubled in bulk. Punch down dough; divide in half. Shape each half into a round 6-inch loaf. Place each loaf in a greased pan; set each filled pan inside another empty ungreased pan. This provides insulation so bottom of loaf doesn't burn. Cover loosely with a dry towel; let rise until doubled in bulk, about 45 minutes. While bread rises, preheat grill with a large fire or use an existing fire. Let fire burn down until it is very hot; spread hot coals in a circle around edge of fire pan. Position a wire rack 4 to 6 inches from heat. With a sharp knife, cut a large 1/2-inch-deep **X** in top of each risen loaf. Place slashed loaves on center of rack. Cover grill; open vents slightly. Bake bread 60 minutes or until well browned. Remove pans to a cooling rack; cool 10 minutes then turn out of pans. Makes 2 round 8- or 9-inch loaves.

Skillet-Grilled Buttermilk Biscuits

Very tender biscuits with a soft, fluffy texture and a slightly sour flavor.

2 cups all-purpose flour
2 teaspoons baking powder
1/2 teaspoon baking soda
1/2 teaspoon salt

1 tablespoon sugar
1/2 cup vegetable shortening
2/3 cup buttermilk

Grease bottom of a 9- or 10-inch cast-iron skillet; set aside. Preheat grill or use an existing hot grill. Fire should be ready as soon as dough is mixed. Arrange hot coals in a circle around edge of fire pan. Position a wire rack 4 to 6 inches from heat. Cover grill; open vents slightly. In a medium bowl, combine flour, baking powder, baking soda, salt and sugar. Using a pastry blender or a fork, cut in shortening until mixture resembles fine, irregular crumbs. Add buttermilk all at once, stirring with a fork only until dough forms a ball. Turn out onto a lightly floured surface; knead 10 to 12 strokes. Pat out dough 1/2 inch thick. Cut biscuits with a floured, round 2-inch cutter. Gather up scraps; pat out again. Cut until all dough is used. Place biscuits, barely touching, in greased skillet. Open grill and quickly set filled skillet on hot grill; immediately replace cover. Bake 20 minutes or until biscuits are puffed, pale golden and cooked through. Turn out of skillet onto a warm platter; serve hot. Makes 16 biscuits.

How to Make Cornmeal-Cinnamon-Raisin Bread

1/Place each round, dough loaf into a greased 8-or 9-inch cake pan. Set each filled cake pan inside another empty, ungreased cake pan, to provide insulation so bottom of loaves don't burn.

2/Cut a large 1/2-inch-deep X in top of each raised loaf. Place loaves on center of barbecue rack. After baking, remove pans to a cooling rack; turn out of pans after 10 minutes.

Gayle's Soft & Buttery Garlic Bread

Everyone loves this soft, moist bread with its buttery cheese topping.

**1/4 cup butter or margarine,
  room temperature**
**1/4 cup Blender Mayonnaise, page 121,
  or other mayonnaise**
2 garlic cloves, minced

**8 French-bread slices,
  1/2 to 1 inch thick**
**3/4 cup finely shredded Cheddar cheese or
  Parmesan cheese or combination (3 oz.)**

Preheat oven broiler. In a small bowl, beat butter or margarine, mayonnaise and garlic until blended; set aside. A few minutes before serving, spread each bread slice with about 1 tablespoon butter mixture. Sprinkle with a generous tablespoon of cheese. Place on a broiler pan; broil 1 to 2 minutes or until cheese is bubbling and lightly browned. Watch closely because it burns easily. Serve immediately. Makes 8 servings.

Grill-Baked Corn Bread

A slightly tangy, very tender corn bread, baked on a covered grill. After barbecuing, the top of this moist bread should look dry, pebbly and pale yellow.

1 egg	1 cup all-purpose flour
2 tablespoons butter or margarine, melted	2 tablespoons sugar
	2 teaspoons baking powder
1 cup buttermilk	1/2 teaspoon baking soda
1 cup yellow cornmeal	1/2 teaspoon salt

Preheat grill or use an existing hot grill; position a wire rack 4 to 6 inches from heat. Grease a 10-inch cast-iron skillet; set aside. In a medium bowl, beat egg, butter or margarine and buttermilk; set aside. In a large bowl, combine cornmeal, flour, sugar, baking powder, baking soda and salt. Add buttermilk mixture all at once to dry ingredients; stir with a fork only until all ingredients are moistened. Pour batter into greased skillet; spread even. Place on rack; cover grill. Bake 15 to 20 minutes or until bread has risen, and a wooden pick inserted in center comes out clean. Remove from grill; cut into 6 wedges. Serve from skillet. Makes about 6 servings.

Variation
Grill-Baked Corn Muffins: Spoon batter into 12 (1/2-inch-diameter) muffin cups, preferably cast-iron. If using lightweight-metal muffin cups, set on a baking sheet on rack to provide insulation so bottoms don't burn. Bake 15 minutes or until muffins have risen, a wooden pick inserted in center comes out clean and tops are dry, pebbled and pale yellow. Remove from muffin cups; serve immediately. Makes 12 muffins.

Cornmeal-Pecan Muffins

These Southern-style muffins are a treat. Be sure to toast the nuts for their full flavor.

1 cup buttermilk	3/4 cup all-purpose flour
1/3 cup vegetable oil	1-3/4 teaspoons baking powder
2 eggs	1 teaspoon baking soda
1-1/4 cups yellow cornmeal	1/4 teaspoon salt
2/3 cup sugar	1 cup coarsely chopped pecans, toasted

Preheat oven to 400F (205C). Grease 12 muffin cups or line with paper liners; set aside. In a medium bowl, beat buttermilk, oil and eggs until blended; set aside. In a large bowl, combine cornmeal, sugar, flour, baking powder, baking soda and salt. Stir pecans into dry mixture. Add buttermilk mixture all at once to dry ingredients; stir with a fork only until all ingredients are moistened. Do not overmix or tunnels will form in baked bread. Spoon batter into prepared muffin cups, filling each about 3/4 full. Bake in preheated oven 12 to 15 minutes or until a wooden pick inserted in center comes out clean. Remove muffins from pan or cups; cool on a wire rack. Makes 12 muffins.

Fluffy Pancakes & Grilled Sausages

Fun to prepare when you're camping at the beach or in the mountains. Serve with butter or margarine and syrup.

1 egg
1-1/4 cups buttermilk
2 tablespoons butter or margarine, melted
1 cup all-purpose flour
1 tablespoon sugar

1 teaspoon baking powder
1/2 teaspoon baking soda
1/4 teaspoon salt
12 pork breakfast sausages
Butter, room temperature

Preheat grill; position a wire rack 4 to 6 inches from heat. In a small bowl, beat egg and buttermilk until blended; stir in butter or margarine. In a medium bowl, combine flour, sugar, baking powder, baking soda and salt. Add buttermilk mixture all at once to dry ingredients; stir only until all ingredients are moistened. Some small lumps will remain in batter. Place a large cast-iron skillet or griddle on one side of rack; grease lightly. Place sausages on other side of rack. Cook 7 to 10 minutes or until browned on all sides, turning frequently. When skillet or griddle is hot enough for a drop of water to bounce across surface, spoon on batter by heaping tablespoons. Cook 1 minute or until edge is dry and surface is full of small holes; turn and cook about 1 minute longer. Remove cooked pancakes to a warm platter. Surround with sausages. Makes 4 servings.

Foil-Wrapped Garlic-Cheese Bread

A hot, crusty loaf with a pungent garlic-cheese butter spread between the slices.

1 unsliced French-bread loaf,
    about 16 inches long,
    4 inches wide
4 to 6 garlic cloves, minced
2-1/2 cups shredded Cheddar cheese
    (about 10 oz.)

1/2 cup butter or margarine,
    room temperature
1/4 teaspoon salt
Several drops hot-pepper sauce
2 tablespoons chopped fresh parsley

Preheat grill or use an existing hot grill; position a wire rack 4 to 6 inches from heat. With a sharp knife, slice French bread at 1-inch intervals, cutting not quite all the way through, so slices remain attached. In a food processor fitted with a metal blade, combine garlic, cheese, butter or margarine, salt, hot-pepper sauce and parsley; process until as smooth as possible. Gently open bread slices; between slices, spread a generous tablespoon of cheese mixture. Wrap loaf tightly in heavy foil or a double thickness of regular foil. About 15 minutes before serving, set foil-wrapped loaf on rack; heat 10 to 15 minutes, turning frequently. Open foil; serve heated loaf from foil or arrange on a warm platter. Makes 8 servings.

DESSERTS

Desserts may not be the climax to a barbecue, but they should leave guests with a satisfied feeling that they have been fed well from start to finish! Because most barbecues are served outdoors, appetites are often still active and ready for a delicious serving of Caramel & Custard Upside-Down Cake, Chocolate-Chocolate Brownies or S'Mores.

Many of these desserts are prepared on the grill—others are baked in an oven. If you plan to serve a completely barbecued meal, we've given you several recipes to choose from. If you want a light fruit dessert that is grilled, serve Grilled Fruit with Sour-Cream Sauce.

Other delicious fruit desserts include Summer-Fruit Sauté and Red, White & Blue Tart. Minted Fresh Fruit for a Crowd is a delicious mixture of fresh fruits with a refreshing citrus-mint dressing. It makes enough to serve a large group for a family reunion or office party.

Our idea of a perfect dessert after a satisfying barbecue is Fresh-Peach Ice Cream; we suggest you try it. Any ice cream is delicious after a barbecue.

Caramel & Custard Upside-Down Cake

Cake, pieces of fruit and a sour-cream custard lie under a crunchy brown-sugar caramel.

1/4 cup butter or margarine
1/2 cup lightly packed brown sugar
6 angel-cake, sponge-cake or pound-cake
  slices, 1/2 to 3/4 inch thick
About 8 canned pear halves,
  well drained

About 16 canned apricot halves,
  well drained
1/2 pint dairy sour cream (1 cup)
2 eggs
1/4 cup granulated sugar
1 teaspoon vanilla extract

Preheat grill or use an existing hot grill, spreading hot coals in a circle around edge of fire box. Position a wire rack 4 to 6 inches from heat to a heatproof surface. On grill or on stovetop, melt butter or margarine in a 10-inch cast-iron skillet. Stir in brown sugar; cook, stirring constantly, until sugar melts and mixture is thick and bubbly. Carefully remove skillet from heat to a heatproof surface; mixture is *very* hot. Cutting and trimming to fit, if necessary, arrange cake slices, slightly overlapping, on hot sugar mixture. Randomly arrange pear and apricot halves, cut-side down, over cake pieces. In a small bowl, combine sour cream, eggs, granulated sugar and vanilla. Pour evenly over fruit layer in skillet. Immediately set skillet on center of rack. Cover grill; bake 30 minutes or until custard is set, caramel bubbles up around edge and mixture has a rich, toasty caramel aroma. Immediately invert cake onto a large round platter, giving a few sharp downward jerks so cake falls in place. Serve warm or at room temperature. Makes 6 to 8 servings.

Sweet 'n Gooey Seven-Layer Bars

A simple bar cookie that can be assembled ahead of time, then baked on the grill.

1 cup graham-cracker crumbs
1/4 cup butter or margarine, melted
1 (6-oz.) pkg. semisweet chocolate pieces
  (1 cup)
1 (6-oz.) pkg. butterscotch-flavored pieces
  (1 cup)

1/2 cup chopped nuts
1 cup shredded coconut
1 (14-oz.) can sweetened condensed milk

Butter an 8-inch-square baking pan; set aside. Pour cracker crumbs into buttered pan; stir in melted butter until blended. Press evenly over bottom of pan; set aside. In a medium bowl, combine remaining ingredients. Spread over cracker crust. Cook immediately; set aside at room temperature up to 1 hour or refrigerate up to 24 hours. Preheat grill or use an existing hot grill, spreading hot coals in a circle around edge of fire box. Position a wire rack 4 to 6 inches from heat. If mixture is refrigerated, bring to room temperature. Set filled pan on center of rack. Cover grill; cook 30 to 45 minutes or until milk mixture turns a deep caramel brown around edges and center is set. Remove to a cooling rack; cool slightly before cutting into 2'' x 1'' bars. Makes 32 bars.

S'Mores

These sweet, gooey treats bring back memories of childhood camp-outs.

4 (1-1/2-oz.) milk-chocolate candy bars   **16 regular marshmallows**
16 graham-cracker squares

Preheat grill or use an existing hot grill. Break chocolate bars in half crosswise. Place 1/2 candy bar on top of each of 8 cracker squares; set aside. Skewer marshmallows; toast 1 or 2 inches from low-glowing coals 2 to 3 minutes, turning every few seconds, until golden and puffy on all sides. Slide 2 hot marshmallows onto each chocolate-topped cracker square; top with another cracker square. Gently press together; eat immediately. Makes 8 servings.

Variation
Robinson Crusoes: These are less sweet but just as gooey. Omit chocolate bars; spread each cracker square with about 1 tablespoon peanut butter. Toast marshmallows as directed above; sandwich between 2 peanut-butter-covered crackers.

Summer-Fruit Sauté

A beautiful dessert! Choose fruits that contrast yet harmonize in color and shape.

Honey Crème Fraîche, see below
2 tablespoons butter or margarine,
   preferably unsalted
1-1/2 to 2 tablespoons sugar
1 teaspoon orange-flavored liqueur,
   or to taste
1 cup sliced strawberries or pitted,
   halved bing cherries

3/4 cup blueberries
1 cup sliced, peeled fresh peaches,
   nectarines, kiwifruit or
   other fresh fruit
Fresh mint leaves, if desired

Honey Crème Fraîche:
1/2 cup whipping cream
   (not ultrapasteurized)

1 teaspoon finely grated lemon peel
1 tablespoon fresh lemon juice
1-1/2 teaspoons honey

Prepare Honey Crème Fraîche; refrigerate until served. In a large sauté pan or skillet, melt butter on stovetop or on a warm grill. Stir in sugar; add liqueur to taste. Add fruits. Cook over medium-low heat, basting with sauce, until fruit is warmed through. Do not overcook. Serve fruit in shallow bowls or on small plates. Serve Honey Crème Fraîche separately. Garnish with mint, if desired. Makes 4 servings.

Honey Crème Fraîche:
In a small bowl, combine whipping cream, lemon peel and lemon juice. Cover with plastic wrap; let stand at room temperature 4 to 6 hours until mixture thickens to consistency of sour cream. Refrigerate until chilled; stir in sugar to taste. Mixture will thicken as it chills. Makes 1/2 cup.

How to Make Grilled Fruit with Sour-Cream Sauce

1/Place pineapple slices and pear halves directly on grill. Barbecue, turning occasionally and brushing with cinnamon mixture.

2/Place lightly grilled fruit on a platter. Pass fruit with a bowl of cool sour-cream sauce. The contrast of hot fruit and cold sauce is a refreshing finale to any barbecued meal.

Grilled Fruit with Sour-Cream Sauce

Pineapple and pears are basted with cinnamon-butter and served with a sour-cream sauce.

Brown Sugar & Sour Cream Sauce, see below
6 tablespoons butter or margarine, melted
1 teaspoon ground cinnamon
6 fresh or well-drained canned pineapple slices packed in its own juices, 1/3 to 1/2 inch thick

3 firm ripe large fresh pears, peeled, halved, cored, or 6 well-drained firm canned pear halves

Brown Sugar & Sour Cream Sauce:
1 pint dairy sour cream (2 cups)
1/2 cup lightly packed brown sugar

1 teaspoon vanilla extract

Prepare Brown Sugar & Sour Cream Sauce; set aside. In a small bowl, combine butter or margarine and cinnamon. Preheat grill or use an existing hot grill; position a wire rack 4 to 6 inches from heat. Place pineapple slices and pear halves on rack. Cook 12 to 15 minutes, turning 2 or 3 times and basting occasionally with cinnamon mixture, until fruit is lightly browned and still slightly firm when pierced with tip of a knife. Remove to a platter. Pour sauce into a small serving bowl; serve separately. Makes 6 servings.

Brown Sugar & Sour Cream Sauce:
In a small bowl, combine sour cream, brown sugar and vanilla. Cover and refrigerate until served. Makes about 2 cups.

Red, White & Blue Tart

Photo on page 69.

Fresh berries star in this show-stopper tart.

Lemon Crème Fraîche, see below
Sweet Crust, see below
3 tablespoons fresh lemon juice
2 tablespoons cornstarch

5 cups blueberries
2/3 cup sugar
1/4 cup water
1 cup fresh raspberries

Lemon Crème Fraîche:
1/2 pint whipping cream (1 cup),
  not ultrapasteurized
Finely grated peel of 1 lemon
  (about 1-1/2 teaspoons)

1 tablespoon fresh lemon juice
Sugar

Sweet Crust:
1 egg yolk
2 tablespoons or more cold water
1-1/2 cups all-purpose flour
1/4 cup sugar

1/2 teaspoon salt
1/2 cup cold, firm unsalted butter,
  cut in 8 pieces

Prepare Lemon Crème Fraîche; refrigerate. Prepare Sweet Crust; set aside. In a small bowl, combine lemon juice and cornstarch; set aside. In a medium saucepan, combine 2 cups blueberries, sugar and water; bring to a boil. Slowly stir in cornstarch mixture; stirring constantly, boil 2 minutes or until thickened. Set aside to cool. Stir 2 cups remaining blueberries into cooled berry mixture; spoon into crust. In a small bowl, combine remaining 1 cup blueberries and raspberries; spoon over top of tart. Blueberry filling, crème fraîche and crust can be made a day ahead. Assemble and refrigerate tart up to 2 hours before serving; let stand at room temperature 10 minutes before serving. Makes 8 to 10 servings.

Lemon Crème Fraîche:
In a small bowl, combine whipping cream, lemon peel and lemon juice. Cover with plastic wrap; let stand at room temperature 4 to 6 hours until mixture thickens to consistency of sour cream. Refrigerate until chilled; stir in sugar to taste. Mixture will thicken as it chills. Makes about 1 cup.

Sweet Crust:
In a small bowl, combine egg yolk and 2 tablespoons water; set aside. In a food processor fitted with a metal blade, combine flour, sugar and salt; process until blended. Add butter; process with on/off motions until mixture resembles coarse crumbs. With motor running, add egg-yolk mixture to flour mixture. Process just until dough begins to hold together. Mixture should still look crumbly, if over processed to the ball stage, crust will be tough. (Or, combine dry ingredients in a medium bowl; cut in butter with a pastry blender or fork. Add egg-yolk mixture. Stir with a fork until pastry begins to form a ball, adding more water, if necessary.) Shape pastry into a ball; flatten slightly. Wrap in plastic wrap; refrigerate at least 30 minutes. Roll out chilled dough on a lightly floured surface to an 11- or 12-inch circle. Fit into a 9- or 10-inch tart pan, 3/4 to 1 inch deep. Trim pastry edge to 1/4 inch above pan. Refrigerate crust at least 30 minutes. Preheat oven to 400F (205C). Prick dough with a fork. Bake blind to prevent shrinkage. To bake blind, line pastry with foil; fill to top with rice, beans or pie weights. Bake crust until side is set, about 15 minutes. Remove foil and rice, beans or pie weights. Bake crust until golden, 15 to 20 minutes. Shield edges of crust with foil during final 10 to 15 minutes of baking, if necessary. Cool completely on a wire rack. Makes 1 (9- or 10-inch) crust.

Fresh-Peach Ice Cream

Cool and refreshing, what could be better than homemade peach ice cream for your barbecue finale?

3 cups finely chopped, peeled
  peaches, (about 6 peaches)
1 tablespoon fresh lemon juice
2/3 cup sugar
2 cups milk

1/2 pint whipping cream (1 cup)
4 egg yolks
1 teaspoon vanilla extract
1/8 teaspoon salt

In a medium bowl, combine peaches, lemon juice and 1/3 cup sugar. Cover and refrigerate 24 hours to form a flavored syrup. Sugar syrup will prevent peaches from freezing solid in ice cream. Use a slotted spoon to drain 1 cup chopped fruit; reserve drained fruit in refrigerator for later addition to ice cream. Pour remaining peaches and syrup into a blender or food processor fitted with a metal blade; process until pureed. Pour into a medium bowl; refrigerate. In a heavy medium saucepan, combine milk, cream, egg yolks, vanilla, salt and remaining 1/3 cup sugar. Stirring constantly, cook over medium heat until thick enough to coat back of a metal spoon, 180F to 185F (80C to 85C). Cool slightly; cover with plastic wrap, pressing plastic wrap on surface of custard. Cool to room temperature; refrigerate until chilled. Stir in peach puree. Process in an ice-cream freezer according to manufacturer's directions. Fold in chopped peaches. Makes about 2 quarts.

Chocolate-Chocolate Brownies

Chocolate pieces make these brownies doubly chocolate and doubly rich.

1 cup butter or margarine
2 oz. unsweetened chocolate
1 cup granulated sugar
1/2 cup all-purpose flour
1 teaspoon baking powder

1/2 cup coarsely chopped walnuts or pecans
2 large eggs
1 teaspoon vanilla extract
1 (6 oz.) pkg. semisweet chocolate pieces (1 cup)
Powdered sugar, if desired

Preheat oven to 375F (190C). Grease an 8- or 9-inch-square baking pan; set aside. Melt butter or margarine and unsweetened chocolate in top of a double boiler or bowl set over hot water. Remove chocolate mixture from heat; stir to blend. Stir in granulated sugar, flour, baking powder and nuts. Beat in eggs and vanilla; stir in chocolate pieces. Spoon batter into greased pan. Bake in preheated oven 20 to 30 minutes or until a wooden pick inserted in center comes out slightly moist. Remove pan to a rack; cool completely in pan. Dust top with powdered sugar, if desired; cut into 9 (3-inch) or 16 (2-inch) squares. Makes 9 squares.

Minted Fresh Fruit for a Crowd

A bounty of summer fruit is piled high in a hollowed-out watermelon or a large glass bowl.

24 cups bite-sized pieces fresh fruit,
  such as berries, kiwifruit, melon
  peaches or grapes
1-1/2 cups fresh orange juice

1/2 cup fresh lemon juice
1/3 cup finely chopped fresh mint
4 to 6 tablespoons sugar
Fresh mint leaves

In a large bowl, combine fruit. In a medium bowl, combine orange juice, lemon juice, chopped mint and sugar; pour over fruit, gently tossing to coat fruit with juice mixture. Cover and refrigerate 2 to 3 hours. Garnish with fresh mint. Makes 24 to 30 servings.

INDEX

Metric Chart

Comparison to Metric Measure

When You Know	Symbol	Multiply By	To Find	Symbol
teaspoons	tsp	5.0	milliliters	ml
tablespoons	tbsp	15.0	milliliters	ml
fluid ounces	fl. oz.	30.0	milliliters	ml
cups	c	0.24	liters	l
pints	pt.	0.47	liters	l

When You Know	Symbol	Multiply By	To Find	Symbol
quarts	qt.	0.95	liters	l
ounces	oz.	28.0	grams	g
pounds	lb.	0.45	kilograms	kg
Fahrenheit	F	5/9 (after subtracting 32)	Celsius	C

Fahrenheit to Celsius

F	C
200—205	95
220—225	105
245—250	120
275	135
300—305	150
325—330	165
345—350	175
370—375	190
400—405	205
425—430	220
445—450	230
470—475	245
500	260

Liquid Measure to Liters

1/4 cup	=	0.06 liters
1/2 cup	=	0.12 liters
3/4 cup	=	0.18 liters
1 cup	=	0.24 liters
1-1/4 cups	=	0.3 liters
1-1/2 cups	=	0.36 liters
2 cups	=	0.48 liters
2-1/2 cups	=	0.6 liters
3 cups	=	0.72 liters
3-1/2 cups	=	0.84 liters
4 cups	=	0.96 liters
4-1/2 cups	=	1.08 liters
5 cups	=	1.2 liters
5-1/2 cups	=	1.32 liters

Liquid Measure to Milliliters

1/4 teaspoon	=	1.25 milliliters		1-1/2 teaspoons	=	7.5 milliliters
1/2 teaspoon	=	2.5 milliliters		1-3/4 teaspoons	=	8.75 milliliters
3/4 teaspoon	=	3.75 milliliters		2 teaspoons	=	10.0 milliliters
1 teaspoon	=	5.0 milliliters		1 tablespoon	=	15.0 milliliters
1-1/4 teaspoons	=	6.25 milliliters		2 tablespoons	=	30.0 milliliters